Narrative
of the Life of Henry Box Brown

{ NARRATIVE }
of the LIFE OF
HENRY BOX
BROWN,
WRITTEN BY HIMSELF

Edited and with an introduction by JOHN ERNEST

The University of North Carolina Press   Chapel Hill

Set in Filosofia and Engravers Bold types
by Tseng Information Systems, Inc.
Manufactured in the United States of America

The paper in this book meets the guidelines for permanence
and durability of the Committee on Production Guidelines for
Book Longevity of the Council on Library Resources.

Library of Congress Cataloging-in-Publication Data
Brown, Henry Box, b. 1816.
Narrative of the life of Henry Box Brown, written by himself /
edited and with an introduction by John Ernest.
p. cm.
ISBN 978-0-8078-3196-0 (cloth : alk. paper)
ISBN 978-0-8078-5890-5 (pbk. : alk. paper)
1. Brown, Henry Box, b. 1816. 2. Fugitive slaves—Virginia—
Biography. 3. African Americans—Virginia—Biography.
4. Slavery—Virginia—History—19th century. 5. African
American abolitionists—Biography. I. Ernest, John. II. Title.
E450.B873 2008
306.3'62092—dc22 [B] 2007047523

Portions of the introduction are drawn from other publications
by the author: "The Reconstruction of Whiteness: William Wells Brown's
The Escape; or, A Leap for Freedom," PMLA 113 (1998): 1108-21, reprinted
by permission of the copyright owner, Modern Language Association of
America; *Liberation Historiography: African American Writers and the Challenge
of History, 1794-1861* (Chapel Hill: University of North Carolina Press, 2004);
"The Family of Man: Traumatic Theology in the *Narrative of the Life of Henry
Box Brown, Written by Himself*," African American Review 41, no. 1 (Spring
2007); "Outside the Box: Henry Box Brown and the Politics of Antislavery
Agency," reprinted by permission of the Arizona Board of Regents from
Arizona Quarterly 63, no. 4 (Winter 2007).

cloth   12 11 10 09 08   5 4 3 2 1
paper   12 11 10 09 08   5 4 3 2 1

CONTENTS

ILLUSTRATIONS

ACKNOWLEDGMENTS

A number of people and institutions have contributed to the preparation of this edition. I am grateful to Sian Hunter, Nathan Mc-Camic, Paul Betz, and Stephanie Wenzel of the University of North Carolina Press for their encouragement and expert guidance. I am indebted as well to the editorial board; the editorial, production, and marketing staffs; and readers Eric Gardner and Joyce-lyn Moody for their thoughtful and detailed suggestions. These readers and editors have helped me considerably in preparing an edition that will be of use and interest to a broad range of readers. I benefited as well from the encouragement and suggestions of Robert S. Levine. As is the case in all of my endeavors, I am especially indebted to Rebecca Mays Ernest for her encouragement, her thoughtful editing and suggestions, and her patience over the time and the distances we've crossed to research, prepare, and proofread this edition.

Various people helped me with the illustrations included in this edition. I am indebted to R. A. Friedman of the Historical Society of Pennsylvania; Edward Gaynor in Special Collections and the Digital Services Staff at the University of Virginia Library; Janie C. Morris of the Rare Book, Manuscript, and Special Collections Library at Duke University; Jackie Penny of the American Antiquarian Society; and Linda Wisniewski of the Library Company of Philadelphia. I'm grateful as well to Nathan McCamic and Paul Betz for their guidance in arranging for and obtaining these illustrations.

Finally, I want to acknowledge my great debt to those few scholars who have done so much to recover and explain the life of Henry Box Brown. I've learned a great deal from the work of William Andrews, R. J. M. Blackett, Daphne A. Brooks, Audrey Fisch, Richard Newman, Cynthia Griffin Wolff, and Marcus Wood. I'm especially indebted, though, to Kathryn Grover's exemplary research in *The Fugitive's Gibraltar: Escaping Slaves and Abolition-*

ism in New Bedford, Massachusetts (Amherst: University of Massachusetts Press, 2001), and to the truly remarkable work of archival research and biographical recovery in Jeffrey Ruggles's *The Unboxing of Henry Brown* (Richmond: The Library of Virginia, 2003). Without Ruggles's work especially, the life and lessons of Henry Box Brown would be, not boxed up, but rather scattered and lost in various archives. This edition would not have been possible without the work of these dedicated scholars.

Narrative
of the Life of
Henry Box
Brown

{ INTRODUCTION

THE EMERGENCE OF

HENRY "BOX" BROWN }

Behind every slave narrative is a significant escape from enslavement, an escape that captured the imaginations of nineteenth-
century readers and audiences. In newspaper accounts, autobiographical narratives, fiction, and drama, and in antislavery
gatherings large and small, people followed the various stories
of individuals who managed to make the difficult journey from
enslavement to relative freedom in the northern United States
and beyond to Canada and England. There was something about
the heroic struggle against the odds that gave point and purpose
to debates over slavery, forcing many to confront the realities of
life under the "peculiar institution" by giving a face, a story, and a
driving spirit to the abstract concept of freedom. British reformer
Harriet Martineau spoke for many when she wrote in 1838 that
"the finest harvest-field of romance perhaps in the world is the
frontier between the United States and Canada." "The vowed stu-
dent of human nature," Martineau suggested, "could not do better
than take up his abode there, and hear what fugitives and their
friends have to tell," for "there have been no exhibitions of the
forces of human character in any political revolution or religious
reformation more wonderful and more interesting than may almost daily be seen there."[1] As Martineau's comments indicate,
one did not need to be a reformer to feel the tug of this story,
and indeed many such students of human nature gathered at the
shores of the slave narratives to explore the various frontiers that
defined the boundaries of freedom in the United States.

For those who had experienced slavery, though, this fascination
with romantic escapes was a mixed blessing, for while the publicity

generated by successful escapes might inspire white Americans to aid in the antislavery cause, it could also alert the authorities about the methods used by the fugitives. The great black abolitionist Frederick Douglass worried about this in his first autobiographical narrative, *Narrative of the Life of Frederick Douglass, an American Slave, Written by Himself* (1845). When Douglass reaches that point in his story when he escaped from slavery, he refuses to offer his reader details. "I have never approved," writes Douglass, "of the very public manner in which some of our western friends have conducted what they call the *underground railroad*, but which, I think, by their open declarations, has been made most emphatically the *uppergroundrailroad*." Those who thus publicize the operations of the Underground Railroad, Douglass asserts, "do nothing towards enlightening the slave, whilst they do much toward enlightening the master."[2] When Douglass returned to this episode in his 1855 revised and expanded autobiography, *My Bondage and My Freedom*, he was more explicit still in his refusal to relate this part of his story: "The practice of publishing every new invention by which a slave is known to have escaped from slavery, has neither wisdom nor necessity to sustain it. Had not Henry Box Brown and his friends attracted slaveholding attention to the manner of his escape, we might have had a thousand *Box Browns* per annum."[3]

Douglass was referring to the subject of the narrative you are about to read, Henry Brown, whose escape from slavery in 1849 became almost immediately one of the most celebrated stories of liberation in the history of American enslavement.[4] Inspired, according to Brown, by God's response to his prayers, Brown placed himself in a crate and had himself shipped by Adams Express from Richmond to Philadelphia, where he was received on March 24, 1849, in the office of the Pennsylvania Anti-Slavery Society. Upon his emergence from the box, Brown sang a song to celebrate the divine inspiration and protection that he believed was central to his success. His story became famous almost immediately. Brown's dramatic escape was a regular presence in antislavery oratory; images of his emergence from the shipping crate were widely circulated and reprinted; his story was soon related in a children's book, *Cousin Ann's Stories for Children* (1849); and reportedly his name was even invoked by a U.S. senator to refer to legislative measures surreptitiously inserted (hidden like Henry Box Brown) into the Compromise of 1850.[5] Brown's story, in short, quickly extended beyond the priorities of antislavery persuasion and became an iconic presence in American culture.

And there it has remained through the twentieth century and into the twenty-first. Accounts of his escape and of his life have been featured in an article published in the *National Geographic* (1984), on a Learning Channel program titled "Great Escapes" (2001), and on the "Living under Enslavement" website of the Henry Ford Museum and Greenfield Village. Reenactments of Brown's escape have been staged; Brown can still be seen emerging from his box at Baltimore's Great Blacks in Wax Museum; and replicas of Brown's box are on display at museums in Virginia and Ontario. He has been the subject of at least one film, more than one opera, various performance pieces, and plays. Moreover, his story (along with the famous image of his emergence from the box) is a regular presence in virtually any presentation on the Underground Railroad, from children's stories to regional and mass-market books. Sometimes the central character, sometimes part of a larger cast of famous "freedom fighters," sometimes the entrance into a sensational story, and sometimes a model of daring political resistance, Henry Box Brown has been and remains a frequent presence in American culture.[6]

Brown's fame might well seem the natural result of an extraordinary and uniquely dangerous mode of escape, but in fact Brown's feat was not all that singular in either its method or its daring. An escape as dangerous and as famous as Brown's was that of William and Ellen Craft, a married couple who traveled from Georgia to Philadelphia by public transportation with Ellen disguised as a white gentleman and her husband playing the role of her (rather, *his*) slave. And there were many such stories, the great majority of which sound nearly impossible or unbearable. Indeed, the great black abolitionist William Still, who witnessed Brown's arrival in the North, noted years later that while "Brown was a man of invention as well as a hero," "his case is no more remarkable than many others. Indeed, neither before nor after escaping did he suffer one-half what many others have experienced."[7] Still was the corresponding secretary and chairman of the Philadelphia Vigilance Committee, and in that role he supported the attempts of various fugitives who had made the difficult journey from the South to the North. After the Civil War, Still gathered his records of these various escapes and published a great many of them in his important book *The Underground Rail Road*, first published in 1872. Included in those records is the story of "William Peel, Alias Box Peel Jones," who escaped by having himself "wrapped in straw and boxed up" in 1859, and the story of an unnamed woman who escaped in a box in 1857, about whom Still states, "She was obviously nearer death than Henry Box Brown, or any of the other box or chest cases that ever came under the notice of the Committee."[8] Indeed, Still pauses early in his record of escapes to emphasize the special challenges that women faced, noting that "females in attempting to escape from a life of bondage undertook three times the risk of failure that males were liable to, not to mention the additional trials and struggles they had to contend with."[9] Still tells of other cases, pointedly using Brown's more famous escape as a point of comparison. Describing the journey of three men "stowed away in a hot berth" on a steamer, in "a space not far from the boiler," with fresh air available to only one man at a time, Still asserts that "Henry Box Brown's sufferings were nothing, compared to what these men submitted to during the entire journey." Still relates as well the story of "one who escaped on the top of a train," a journey "more perilous than the way William and Ellen Craft, or Henry Box Brown traveled."[10]

With so many tales of escape to be told, how did Brown's rise to such a level of fame, becoming one of the primary stories associated with the history of both slavery and the Underground Railroad? The plan, of course, was to keep it secret, to protect both Brown and those who had helped him. James Miller McKim, a white abolitionist and agent of the Pennsylvania Anti-Slavery Society who had helped facilitate Brown's escape, had admonished his colleagues that Brown's feat should not be publicized. But an article published in the Vermont *Burlington Courier* and reprinted in the *New York Daily Tribune* just weeks after the event made the story public, though with no names mentioned. The antislavery press soon followed suit, and Brown became known to those sympathetic to the antislavery cause. The following month, May 1849, Brown, who had been moved to Boston and then New Bedford, Massachusetts, for his own safety, attended the New England Anti-Slavery Convention, where his story was mentioned during the opening session. That evening, Brown was introduced to the convention audience by another famous fugitive Brown, William Wells Brown, who jokingly referred to Henry Brown as "Boxer." The next evening, Brown was again brought to the stage, this time to sing the "Hymn of Thanksgiving" that he had sung upon his emergence from the box in Philadelphia. By the end of the convention, the name Henry "Box" Brown was firmly in place, and its bearer was a public speaker and performer in the antislavery cause.[11]

To a great extent, Brown himself promoted his story and crafted his own fame, from the song he sang when he emerged from his box to the career he launched after his story became public knowledge. In the summer of 1849, Brown began making public appearances at various meetings in New England; by June, his appearances included a printed version of the song he regularly sang at those meetings, illustrated with an "Engraving of the Box." Soon, a second song sheet was printed—this one a rewriting of a racist, blackface minstrel tune (Stephen Foster's "Old Uncle Ned")—that told the story of Brown's escape, and again including an engraving of a box.[12] By September, Brown had produced a book, the narrative of his life written by the white abolitionist and printer Charles Stearns, and for a month after the publication of the book Brown and Stearns together toured the region to promote it. By the end of the year of his escape, Brown was planning to use some of the profits from his book to create a moving panorama that would place his escape within the larger story of slavery and that would further distinguish his public appearances. The panorama, *Henry Box Brown's Mirror of Slavery*, was a series of paintings on a sheet of canvas reported to be 50,000 feet long that would be gradually unwound to reveal successive scenes related to Brown's personal experience and to the history of slavery and the slave trade.[13] It premiered in Boston in April 1850. By 1851 Brown was a well-known abolitionist and public figure living in England, where he not only continued his presentations of the panorama but also staged a reenactment of his escape. In England he was shipped from Bradford to Leeds, where his arrival was "preceded by a band of music and banners, representing the stars and stripes of America, paraded through the principle streets of the town."[14] It was in England as well that Brown published the dramatically revised version of his narrative reprinted here, this one more focused on the songs and stories he related on the public stage. Brown's rise to fame, in short, was quite deliberate as Brown discovered both the political and the professional opportunities available in antislavery circles.

But for all his fame, the story of Brown's life has remained relatively unknown, and the two narratives of his life and escape have been unavailable to most readers until relatively recently. The nature and extent of the interest in Brown is aptly indicated by the long title of his first narrative, promising a story of a man "Who Escaped from Slavery Enclosed in a Box 3 Feet Long and 2 Wide." Those interested in the Underground Railroad, along with most students of African American history, have heard of Brown, but their knowledge of his life rarely extends beyond his famous escape—and as his adopted name suggests, most people find it difficult to talk about Brown without focusing on the dimensions of his shipping crate and on his life-threatening journey from slavery to the relative and partial freedom he found in the North and, later, in England. Absent from such accounts is the reality of his experiences under slavery, of the wife and children Brown left behind, the family sold away from him, and the home to which he could not return. Indeed, absent from such accounts is the larger story of the many people left behind, the communities of the enslaved. The freedom celebrated in Brown's name is a freedom that fails to account for the systemic and ongoing injustices of America's "peculiar institution," and that fails to account as well for the deeply racist culture in which he found himself even after he arrived in the North.

Brown himself can seem to downplay the importance of his life before his escape. At the beginning of his 1851 *Narrative*, he warns readers not to expect a dramatic story of physical oppression. "The tale of my own sufferings," he states, "is not one of great interest to those who delight to read of hair-breadth adventures, of tragical occurrences, and scenes of blood:—my life, even in slavery, has been in many respects comparatively comfortable." But of course this is the point, for those who experienced slavery understood what mere spectators and sympathizers sometimes fail to see. As Saidiya Hartman, one of the best scholars of slavery, puts it, "Shocking displays too easily obfuscate the more mundane and socially endurable forms of terror."[15] While Brown's life included "tragical occurrences" and "shocking displays," the greater terror of his story has to do with the extent to which the system of slavery shaped the lives of the enslaved and the enslavers alike. In the nineteenth century, audiences who heard Brown speak knew that a central part of his story involved the loss of his wife and children.[16] Beyond the nineteenth century, though, attention to Brown's story has focused primarily on his escape, even on the dimensions of the box itself, and on his subsequent career as a public lecturer and performer.

While Brown's escape is often considered to be unique, his full story is representative of many lives lived in enslavement. He was born, sometime around 1815, in Louisa County, Virginia, where his parents, four sisters, and three brothers were all enslaved to John Barret, a tobacco farmer. His parents were deeply religious, and his owner, in the absurd scale of things under the system of slavery, was comparatively kind. But by the time Brown reached his early teens, Barret had hired an overseer whose harsh treatment confronted Brown with the capricious realities of slavery. When John Barret died in 1830, Brown's family was divided among several owners. Brown was sent to work in the tobacco factory of his new owner, William Barret, in Richmond, Virginia, where Brown was under the supervision of a black overseer, Wilson Gregory, the first of a succession of overseers that Brown encountered in Richmond, most of whom, unlike Gregory, treated the slaves harshly. In Richmond, Brown went to First Baptist Church, which many African Americans attended. There he met an enslaved woman, Nancy, whom he married in 1836, though under the system of slavery their marriage was unrecognized and unprotected by law.

As was the case for many others born in similar circumstances, Brown's marriage emphasized the tragic instabilities of life under the system of slavery. Nancy Brown was owned by Hancock Lee, who sold Nancy to an abusive couple, Joseph H. and Mary Colquitt, a year after she and Henry were married. In an episode that Brown relates in the 1851 *Narrative*, Joseph Colquitt became ill around 1844 and asked the slaves, Brown included, to pray for him. Later, when Colquitt felt humiliated by his request, he whipped many of his own slaves and, Brown believed, decided to sell Brown's wife and children to Samuel Cottrell simply out of spite. Short of the selling price by $50, Cottrell offered Brown his assurances that he would not sell Nancy to anyone else on the condition that Brown would provide the remaining money for the sale, money that Brown earned by extra labor. Although untrusting, Brown had little choice but to agree to the deal. Immediately after the purchase, however, Cottrell presented Brown with new demands that Brown must provide housing for his family and also pay $50 a year for the time lost when Nancy cared for her small children. In August 1848, Cottrell demanded more money from Brown, which Brown was unable to provide. Brown's children and his wife, pregnant with their fourth child, were sold that day. Brown appealed to his own master for help but was sharply refused and informed that he could acquire another wife. Shortly after, Brown watched as his wife and children were led away in a slave coffle, headed south, purchased by a Methodist preacher from North Carolina.

The loss of his family eventually led Brown to his decision to escape, a journey that began with a break from religion and that ended with a jubilant hymn of thanksgiving upon his arrival in the

North. Brown had been an active member of First Baptist Church in Richmond, which included both white and black congregants. In 1841, the white members built a new church, in which African Americans were not allowed without special permission, and they sold the old building to the black congregants, who worked hard to come up with the $3,000 price. The old church, now the First African Baptist Church, was overseen by a white governing board and led by a white preacher and was obviously restricted in its message to its congregants.[17] Still, Brown was a proud member of the choir and leading member of the congregation for many years. But when his family was sold away from him, Brown refused to attend the church until he was coaxed back for a special benefit concert for the church on Christmas Day, 1848. While performing in that concert, Brown could not suppress his anger at being forced to contribute to the system of slavery, and he thereupon broke his relation to the choir and the church.

The experience made Brown determined to escape from his condition. In 1849, he sought help from a Massachusetts-born white man, Samuel Smith, who might have been involved in another escape attempt; Smith was also a man who needed money. Brown offered to pay for Smith's assistance, and with the help of a former fellow choir member, James C. A. Smith, Brown worked on a plan, eventually suggesting his famous method of escape. Samuel Smith went to Philadelphia to arrange for the reception of the box. After correspondence, hesitations, and delays, the box was addressed to James Johnson, 131 Arch Street, in Philadelphia, and was shipped on March 23, 1849. After a very difficult journey of more than twenty-four hours, the box was delivered to the antislavery office in Philadelphia, and shortly after it was opened, Brown sang a thanksgiving hymn he had prepared for the occasion, based on Psalm 40: "I waited patiently for the Lord; and he inclined unto me, and heard my cry. He brought me up also out of a horrible pit, out of the miry clay, and set my feet upon a rock, and established my goings. And he hath put a new song in my mouth, even praise unto our God: many shall see it, and fear, and shall trust in the Lord."

The World of Antislavery Culture

When Henry Box Brown arrived in the North, he entered a culture defined by racism and torn by debates not only over slavery but also over the antislavery movement. The ideals celebrated in the Declaration of Independence and proclaimed at every Fourth of July celebration were, at best, only selectively applied to many people born and raised in the United States—and were, at worst, violated in almost every arena of political, economic, religious, and social life. This was true in the North as well as in the South, and in churches as well as in legislative halls. Hosea Easton, for example, an early African American leader, had grown up witnessing continued efforts to restrict his family's position in Massachusetts churches—including denial of a seat among the whites, tarring of the pew that the family had purchased, and even bodily removal when the family refused to relinquish their position.[18] This was by no means an isolated example of the harassment and physical abuse that African Americans experienced in the North. Indeed, white mobs threatened the safety of northern blacks regularly. In 1834, for example, white mobs in Philadelphia physically attacked black individuals, destroyed a number of houses, and burned the New African Hall and Presbyterian church. Those involved in the antislavery movement were regularly attacked as well. William Lloyd Garrison, the white abolitionist and publisher of one of the most influential of the antislavery newspapers, was publicly harassed and paraded through the streets of Boston at the end of a rope in 1835. Proslavery mobs rioted regularly—in Philadelphia (where mobs continued to burn buildings associated with African American and antislavery organizations); in New York City in 1834; in Utica, New York, in 1835; in Cincinnati, Ohio, in 1836; and elsewhere. In 1836, the federal House of Representatives adopted a gag rule prohibiting the reception of antislavery petitions and restricting congressional debate. In 1837, one white abolitionist, Marius Robinson, was kidnaped, tarred, and feathered, while another, Elijah Lovejoy, was murdered by a mob in Alton, Illinois. Two decades later, in 1856, white senator Charles Sumner was physically attacked and seriously injured by Representative Preston Brooks of South Carolina while sitting at his desk in the Capitol. The battles over slavery, and over the definition of the nation's character, were both political and personal, both philosophical and physical, leading eventually to civil war.[19]

Resistance to slavery was as established and as various as the mechanisms of the system of slavery itself. For those still enslaved, resistance could mean feigned incompetence, disruption of daily life, escape, or armed revolt. In a national convention of African Americans in 1843, the great black abolitionist Henry Highland Garnet presented a provocative speech encouraging the slaves of the South to resist the system as a matter of moral duty. "There is not much hope of redemption," Garnet argued, "without the shedding of blood. If you must bleed, let it all come at once—rather *die freemen than live as slaves*."[20] By the time Garnet presented that address, he had a rich heritage of examples of heroic and determined resistance from which to draw. The best-known conspiracies (which were exposed before they could be completed) were those of Gabriel Prosser in Virginia (1800) and Denmark Vesey in South Carolina (1822); the best-known revolt was the one led by Nat Turner in Virginia (1831). These conspiracies and revolts, while unsuccessful, left their mark on American culture, inspiring heated debates over slavery and tremendous anxiety among the slaveholders. Important also was the rebellion in 1839 on the Spanish slavery ship *Amistad*, an event that led to legal disputes, political skirmishes, and eventually a Supreme Court decision in 1841 to grant the rebels their freedom. In 1841, another rebellion occurred upon the slaver *Creole*, during which the slaves took the ship to the British colony of Nassau and attained their freedom. While northern African Americans were divided on the practicality and wisdom of Garnet's advice to the slaves, it cannot be doubted that the various forms of slave resistance destabilized the system of slavery, if only by increasing the anxiety and forcing the hand of slaveholders who claimed that slavery was a paternal and benevolent institution.

At the beginning of the 1830s, significant developments in response to both slavery and racism led to a new and more complex era of antislavery activity. In 1829 David Walker published his uncompromising *Appeal to the Coloured Citizens of the World*, noting that by doing so he had put his life in danger. Walker's *Appeal* was a strongly worded and militant manifesto designed to rouse black solidarity and resistance to slavery and to white supremacy, both in the South and in the North. Southern whites protested the publication strongly and tried to prevent it from entering the South (though the book was smuggled in). When David Walker was found dead shortly after the publication of the third edition of the *Appeal* in 1830, many of that time and since suspected that Walker's death was connected with reactions to the appeal.[21] In 1831 Nat Turner's insurrection in Southampton County, Virginia, led slaveholders to fear the possibility of organized revolt in other areas of the South. Many white antislavery advocates, in turn, worried about the violence of Walker's discourse and of Turner's actions, and their concerns led them to question their alliance to antislavery forces. Important, too, was the launching of William Lloyd Garrison's antislavery newspaper the *Liberator* at that same time—a paper in which a newly insistent and uncompromising abolitionist voice found a prominent and influential forum. In 1832, the New England Anti-Slavery Society was formed in Boston; in 1833, the American Anti-Slavery Society was founded in Philadelphia; in 1839, the antislavery Liberty Party was formed.

The antislavery movement became increasingly active and influential, if often divided on matters of philosophy and methods. The Liberty Party, for example, opposed Garrison's refusal to participate in politics and his call for the dissolution of the Union. Resistance to some of Garrison's methods and principles led to a break in the American Anti-Slavery Society in 1840, resulting in the formation of the anti-Garrisonian American and Foreign Anti-Slavery Society. But beyond the divisions were strong alliances, and in spite of the divisions the antislavery movement was a growing force in national and international politics and culture. Through lecturers who traveled from town to town (often at some risk to their personal safety), antislavery newspapers and books, conventions and political movements, and other forums, the antislavery movement forced the issue of slavery as a defining institution of American national life.

By the 1850s, both ethical and political pressures brought the issue to the forefront of national life, as proslavery and anti-slavery tensions became increasingly heated, and as divisions between the northern and southern states made civil war seem increasingly inevitable. The decade began with the Compromise of 1850, an attempt to resolve sectional conflicts that served largely to heighten them. The compromise included an updated and strengthened Fugitive Slave Act—an act that, many north-erners argued, required all American citizens to become slave catchers. The law placed the issue of runaway slaves under fed-eral jurisdiction, allowing federal commissioners to force citi-zens to aid in the recapture of slaves who reached the North while also denying fugitive slaves trial by jury or the right to testify on their own behalf. A revealing detail of this law is that the federal commissioners who oversaw this process were paid five dollars if they decided in favor of the black person in question, but they were paid ten dollars if they "returned" the alleged fugitive to a slaveholder. Many fugitive slaves left for Canada or England fol-lowing the passage of this law, as did many African Americans in the North who either wanted to join their fugitive relatives or feared for their own security in a nation that did not recognize or protect their rights.

To be sure, both white and black northerners resisted this law. Large mobs formed in Boston to protest the reenslavement of Thomas Sims in 1851 and Anthony Burns in 1854, two of the most famous and, for the federal government, expensive of these cases. In 1851 a determined gathering met a band of slave catchers in Christiana, Pennsylvania, and forced them to retreat; in that same year a large number of black and white protesters (some estimate the number to be as high as 10,000) stormed a court-room in Syracuse, New York, and rescued a fugitive slave, William "Jerry" Henry. The year 1858 saw the famous Oberlin-Wellington rescue, in which Professor Simon M. Bushnell and a group of students (black and white) from Oberlin College, Ohio, came to the aid of a fugitive named John Price. Many of those involved in these efforts suffered for their actions, but the fame of these episodes was preserved carefully in the pages of the antislavery press.[22]

The national determination to preserve and protect the system of slavery was great, however, and these local confrontations were a prelude to a larger battle for political and ideological control over the nation's future. The Compromise of 1850 was followed by other measures that added to the violations of African American rights and civil security. In 1854, Congress approved the Kansas-Nebraska Act, which allowed voting citizens of those regions (and the vote was, of course, restricted) to determine themselves whether their territory would enter the Union as a slave or a free state. This act led to increased violence in the territories and contributed to the formation of the Republican Party as an antislavery political force. In 1857, the Supreme Court announced its decision in the case of *Dred Scott v. Sanford*, in which Chief Justice Roger B. Taney declared that African Americans had no rights that white Americans were obligated to respect. The political and ideological debates that followed this decision helped to further define the already sharp divisions that were driving the nation toward open conflict. When John Brown led his group of black and white soldiers in the raid at Harpers Ferry, Virginia, in 1859, what had long been an open if localized war became sharply focused. John Brown became a white martyr to a cause that had, by this time, a long history of soldiers and martyrs. In that year, the *Anglo-African Magazine*, an African American publication in New York, published the public reports of an early revolutionary with those of a later one, placing Nat Turner next to John Brown, black militancy next to white, and called for Americans to recognize the inevitable struggle ahead and to decide what role they would play in that conflict.[23] The time had come, argued many, to complete the still-unfinished work of the American Revolution.

The Black Atlantic and the White World

The escape from slavery—both the personal experience of slavery and the racial system of slavery—involved a journey that extended beyond the borders separating the American South and North, and very often those who had managed to travel from the American South found themselves journeying farther to England and Africa. Paul Gilroy—looking back at the terrible journeys, the middle passage, that once brought Africans to enslavement, and looking forward for an understanding capable of accounting for the dispersed representatives of the African diaspora—formulated what has proven to be an influential concept, that of the Black Atlantic. Gilroy means the term to draw our attention to "the image of ships in motion across the spaces between Europe, America, Africa, and the Caribbean," because "ships immediately focus attention on the middle passage, on the various projects for redemptive return to an African homeland, on the circulation of ideas and activists as well as the movement of key cultural and political artifacts: tracts, books, gramophone records, and choirs."[24] Like most of the enslaved people of his generation, Henry Box Brown had never experienced the middle passage. But he had inherited both the challenges and the responsibilities that followed from it, and soon after his escape, he participated significantly in "the circulation of ideas" and "the movement of key cultural and political artifacts" through his public appearances and his writing both in the United States and in England.

As was the case with Brown, the antislavery movement provided a forum for many activists who became important figures in American history, and the public stage available to these activists was extensive—indeed, transatlantic. There was significant support for the antislavery movement in Great Britain, for example, and many African Americans traveled there to give lectures, meet with supporters, and raise funds for the cause back in the states. Often, too, what has been called the "black abolitionist mission to the British Isles" was a matter of more immediate necessity, as many of those who were, in the United States, still "fugitive slaves" by law went abroad in order to avoid recapture.[25] "Between 1830 and 1865," C. Peter Ripley has observed, "black abolitionists left universities, newspaper offices, cabinet shops, pulpits, and plantations for the British Isles. Some boarded the best Cunard Line ships after elaborate farewell gatherings; others sneaked out of the American and Canadian harbors just ahead of slave catchers."[26] Frederick Douglass's freedom was purchased while he was in England, as was William Wells Brown's, and both men took advantage of their time there to lecture widely. Brown published some of his most important books while in England, and it was in England that William and Ellen Craft published their own version of their famous story. Though he had never been enslaved, Charles Lenox Remond traveled to London to represent the antislavery cause, as did his sister Sarah Parker Remond. But those who had experienced slavery firsthand were especially in demand by British audiences, and those who had escaped slavery but not American law went to England with particular urgency. As Audrey Fisch has observed, "For black Americans in the abolitionist campaign in England, the stakes were fairly clear: personal safety and personal ambition translated readily into public politics." "All of this," Fisch adds, "came to a climax in 1850 with the passage of the Fugitive Slave Law, which rendered the Northern states of the US and even Canada unsafe for those fleeing slavery."[27]

But African Americans went abroad as well because the American antislavery movement was deeply influenced by the methods that had proven so influential in Great Britain some years earlier. Indeed, as their significant publications in England suggest, African American abolitionists benefited from established antislavery traditions that influenced their approaches to oration, narrative, poetry, fiction, and other written and oral approaches to representing their cause and drawing the support of audiences. In his study of eighteenth-century British abolitionism, Brycchan Carey notes that while "almost all the major political questions of the day were discussed in sentimental terms[,] . . . none gave rise to quite as much sentimental rhetoric as the debate over slavery and abolition."[28] Central to the British abolitionist movement,

Carey notes, was "the rhetoric of sensibility," which provided "an opportunity to tap directly into the heart of the human condition."[29] But even beyond writing devoted directly to the abolitionist cause, many scholars believe that the pervasive realities of the slave trade influenced, directly and indirectly, the literary and philosophical investigations of British—and, later, American—Romantic writers. "The African presence," claims scholar Debbie Lee, "shaped the British Romantic imagination. Because slavery was such an intimate part of the imagination, writers produced works so distinct that an entire literary period formed around them."[30]

The reciprocal and dynamic influences of antislavery and Romantic thought helped to prepare readers and audiences for the antislavery message and, indeed, helped to promote the antislavery cause, as "the rhetoric of sensibility" provided the common language necessary to organized and practical social reform efforts. "One does not have to look very far," Dwight A. McBride suggests, "to discover that the ties between racialized discourse and Romanticism not only exist but are, in fact, quite abundant."[31] Consider, for example, McBride's overview of dual courses of literary Romanticism and British and American abolitionism:

> Literary Romanticism in England (roughly 1789 to 1832) coincides with the rise of British abolitionism (the Society for the Abolition of the Slave Trade was formed in 1787) and the fierce parliamentary debates over the cessation of England's participation in the international slave trade, which ended in the passage of the Abolition Bill in 1807. This act was followed by the passage of the Emancipation Bill in 1833. In the United States, literary Romanticism (roughly 1836 to 1865) is nearly concurrent with the formation of the American Anti-Slavery Society (1833) and the rise of the Garrisonian variety of abolitionism, culminating in the epic conflict of the Civil War.[32]

As McBride observes, "The concerns of abolitionism (marked by the organizations in Britain, France, and the United States that first appeared in the late eighteenth century to address the problem of slavery), were transatlantic and transgeneric."[33] It is hardly surprising, then, that nineteenth-century African American abolitionist writers addressed a transatlantic range of readers. Out of existing literary traditions, African American writers forged their own approach to abolitionist writing that was at once familiar and challenging to readers of white-authored novels, essays, histories, poetry, and orations. Because they were able to both draw from and modify existing rhetorical and political traditions, many African American men and women discovered in the antislavery movement opportunities to rise to prominence.

But while African Americans within the movement found many great allies and true friends, both at home and abroad, they could never afford to forget their unstable position in a culture devoted to the rights and privileges of white men. Indeed, even when they worked toward northern uplift, African American writers and activists recognized that white supremacy was the unspoken assumption even among those white reformers who were their most fervent allies. As early as 1837, historian Leon Litwack has noted, "when the *Colored American* reviewed the economic plight of the Negro in the wake of the Panic of 1837, it noted that not one local abolitionist had placed a Negro in any conspicuous position in his business establishment; in fact, it could not even find a Negro in the offices of the New York Anti-Slavery Society."[34] And as William H. and Jane H. Pease have noted, much of what white abolitionists said and did "betrayed an implicit and at times explicit belief in racial inferiority." Edmund Quincy, for example, "lashed out in a letter to Caroline Weston in 1846 at 'Wendell's nigger,' whom he held responsible for botching an Antislavery Report," and "as late as 1860 Theodore Parker, a backer of John Brown, observed [in a letter published in 1860] that 'the Anglo-Saxon with common sense does not like this Africanization of America; he wishes the superior race to multiply rather than the inferior.'"[35]

This situation only added to the appeal of addressing messages to American readers from abroad, a frequent presence in the antislavery press. Black abolitionists such as William Wells Brown and Martin R. Delany delighted in contrasting regularly and with force their public reception and treatment in the United States with that they enjoyed in England, where they reported pointedly not only on their meetings with prominent white public figures but also the gracious treatment they received in hotels or on public transportation. But while they told a true story, they did not always relate the full story. As Douglas A. Lorimer has observed, even in England "neither black speakers nor their subjects were free from ridicule and abuse," and African Americans abroad sometimes faced "outright discrimination."[36] In short, black abolitionists faced both a world of opportunities and a world of challenges in negotiating the transatlantic waters of the white antislavery world, and they frequently responded by playing each side against the other in their speeches and their written works.

Certainly, such negotiations played a central role in Henry Box Brown's antislavery efforts in England, but that other and more famous Brown, William Wells Brown, was particularly adept at shifting his message to account for the dynamics of transatlantic antislavery sympathy. Like many antislavery writers and speakers, Brown referred to Great Britain as the political body that embraced the principles associated with the United States. He noted, for example, in an 1854 speech that "while Slavery has been gaining ground in America, Liberty has been marching onward in Great Britain," and that "monarchical England has done that which Republican America refuses to do for humanity."[37] In September of that same year, Brown had tried to position northern antislavery efforts more specifically, drawing the distinction between American and English antislavery efforts rather differently. The antislavery organization in England, he argued, is "so inactive, it scarcely does any thing throughout the year but hold an anniversary meeting." "Speeches like those which were made in the Conference to-day," Brown added for his American audience, "would not be tolerated on the platform of the British and Foreign Anti-Slavery Society in London."[38] Identifying the U.S. antislavery movement as both behind and ahead of Great Britain in antislavery activity, Brown used transatlantic ties and distances to challenge audiences on both sides of the ocean.

At times, though, an even more direct statement of the racial politics within the antislavery movement seemed necessary, as

Frederick Douglass emphasized when commenting on a letter from the Reverend Samuel Ringgold Ward published in *Frederick Douglass' Paper* in April 1855. Noting that "we look upon the past as a precedent for the future," Douglass supported Ward's public declaration of frustration with white antislavery allies:

> Our oppressed people are wholly ignored, in one sense, in the generalship of the movement to effect our Redemption. Nothing is done—no, nothing, as our friend Ward asserts, to inspire us with the Idea of our Equality with the whites. We are a poor, pitiful, dependent and servile class of Negroes, "*unable to keep pace*" with the movement, to which we have adverted—not even capable of "*perceiving what are its demands, or understanding the philosophy of its operations!*" Of course, if we are "unable to keep pace" with our white brethren, in their vivid perception of the demands of our cause, those who assume the leadership of the Anti-Slavery Movement; if it is regarded as having "*transcended our ability*," we cannot consistently expect to receive from those who indulge in this opinion, a *practical recognition of our Equality*. This is what we are contending for. It is what we have never received. It is what we must receive to inspire us with confidence in the self-appointed generals of the Anti-Slavery host, the Euclids who are *theoretically* working out the almost insoluble problem of our future destiny.[39]

Douglass put it even more plainly in 1856, in an article titled "The Alliance of Negro Hate and Anti-Slavery": "Opposing slavery and hating its victims has come to be a very common form of Abolitionism."[40] To follow the trail of a slave narrative north to "freedom," in short, can give one a false sense of completion, for other journeys awaited, and freedom, in its legal recognitions and in its daily manifestations, remained elusive.[41]

In response to the pressures of a white supremacist culture, then, African American communities worked on all fronts, at home and abroad, to improve their situation and to provide the foundations necessary for future generations to rise from the shadows and to make what we commonly call the American dream a reality and not just a set of selective opportunities and an ideological cover for systemic oppression. African Americans, often with the support of white allies, formed fraternal and religious organizations that became important centers of political and economic life; they formed libraries and educational societies; they fought, often physically, for equal access to everything from theaters to public transportation; they held state and national conventions to determine and coordinate collective action; they published newspapers, pamphlets, orations, poems, essays, novels, plays, and histories in which they advocated forcefully for social change while correcting the textual representations and historical accounts that placed those of African descent in an inferior and dependent position; and they built schools, developed educational approaches designed to counter the inadequacies of the education their children were receiving, and lobbied for the integration of the schools of the white populations. Many African Americans were highly educated and accomplished scholars and writers; some were wealthy; and many were leaders in the ongoing cause of liberty and human rights. Still, they met with resistance on all fronts. White supremacist publications and popular culture (including that most popular form of entertainment, the minstrel show) created an image of African American character in the popular mind that was quite influential. Economic opportunities were limited, and labor organizations created white working-class solidarity on the backs of African Americans. Educational opportunities were denied. Special legislation was enacted in Connecticut, for example, to undermine the efforts of an interracial school, and in New Hampshire an interracial school was physically dragged from its foundation.[42]

In short, African Americans enjoyed a transatlantic world within which they could make themselves heard, but they faced as well obstinate local, state, and national restrictions on the opportunities they could expect for themselves, their families, and their communities. Both the broad opportunities and the strict limitations of their situation influenced their approaches to the antislavery cause—and complicated the task of presenting their stories as testimony to their cause, be it orally on the stage or in writing on the printed page. When Henry Box Brown recorded his own story for publication, then, one significant question he faced was "How secure was this new box, this narrative of his life, and would the story he needed to tell survive the journey?"

⊰⊱

Narrative of the Life of Henry Box Brown, Written by Himself

The narratives of the formerly enslaved entered a complex, divisive, and racist culture, and of course this culture had an effect on the art and reception of the narratives themselves. Indeed, African Americans who had endured and escaped from slavery knew well what would capture the attention of their audiences. In an 1847 speech to an antislavery society, for example, William Wells Brown told his audience, "I may try to represent to you Slavery as it is; another may follow me and try to represent the condition of the Slave; we may all represent it as we think it is; and yet we shall all fail to represent the real condition of the Slave." The problem was and remains that, in part, "the real condition of the Slave" was virtually unrepresentable. Language seems inadequate, and any story that one can tell seems almost to diminish the enormousness of the subject and dishonor those whose lives were most directly controlled by the system of slavery. But the problem, as Brown noted in that same speech, is also one of audience—what one's audience is prepared to hear, and how the story will be received by that audience. Considering the possibility of trying to represent "the real condition of the Slave," Brown told his audience, "Your fastidiousness would not allow me to do it; and if it would, I, for one, should not be willing to do it;—at least to an audience. Were I about to tell you the evils of Slavery, to represent to you the Slave in his lowest degradation, I should wish to take you, one at a time, and whisper it to you."[43] Following these remarks, one can imagine the audience leaning closer as Brown presented a speech that indeed addressed the horrors of slavery but that focused more directly on the effects of slavery on white American character.

In fact, readers were drawn to narratives of enslavement regardless of any fastidiousness they might claim, for slave narratives were quite popular, and slave narrators seemed to understand what descriptions of slavery were most likely to grab the attention of their white northern readers.[44] In an 1849 article published in the *Christian Examiner*, for example, the Reverend Ephraim Peabody, a white Unitarian minister of Boston, identifies slave narratives as "a new department" of "the literature of civilization." "There are those," Peabody states, "who fear lest the elements of poetry and romance should fade out of the tame and monotonous social life of modern times. There is no danger of it while there are any slaves left to seek for freedom, and to tell the story of their efforts to obtain it."[45] For Peabody, the slave narratives offered powerful testimony to "the necessary evils of this mournful institution"—that is, the evils encouraged, perpetuated, and rationalized by persons whose interest it was to maintain the system of slavery. Similarly, Lucius C. Matlack's introduction to another well-known story of enslavement and escape, *Narrative of the Life and Adventures of Henry Bibb, an American Slave, Written by Himself*, indicates the benevolent adventure readers expected to experience through these narratives. "Naturally and necessarily, the enemy of literature," Matlack asserts, American slavery has provided "the prolific theme of much that is profound in argument, sublime in poetry, and thrilling in narrative. . . . Gushing fountains of poetic thought, have started from beneath the rod of violence, that will long continue to slake the feverish thirst of humanity outraged, until swelling to a flood it shall rush with wasting violence over the ill-gotten heritage of the oppressor."[46] Matlack does not seem to entertain the possibility that "the ill-gotten heritage of the oppressor" might be a phrase that encompasses white antislavery sympathizers as well as southern slaveholders. But African American writers, well versed in the racism in the North generally and in the antislavery movement specifically, understood that they faced a challenge of telling truths beyond what white audiences were prepared to hear or understand.

Certainly, there was a ready audience for Henry Box Brown's story, and Brown was a quick study in the attractions of a dramatic and entertaining presentation. But he used his already famous story strategically. Many readers of both versions of his narrative have noted that Brown's claim to fame, the dramatic escape that provided him with his middle name, plays a relatively minor role in his 1849 narrative and a decidedly minor role in the 1851 version. Brown understood, in other words, that his escape was a way to draw readers and audiences into a larger story, including an account of "the more mundane and socially endurable forms of terror" that were a regular presence in the lives of the enslaved.[47] Brown understood as well that he had other stories to tell—of marriage and family, of spiritual struggles in and beyond established religious institutions, and of friendship, trust, and community as well as of friendships lost, trust betrayed, and communities broken and forsaken. He needed to tell of a "comparatively comfortable" life without giving readers cause to think that slavery was or could be an acceptable institution. He needed to get beyond the horrors that call for sympathy to represent a network of economic, political, religious, and social practices and codes of conduct that together, regardless of comparative comforts or horrific violations, made for an unstable foundation for a nation that claimed devotion to political liberty and Christian ideals. In many ways, he needed to tell a story for which there were no adequate words, a story beyond what his readers and audiences expected to encounter and knew how to understand. He needed to address a philosophical and practical realm of the American social order for which there was no single moral, no immediate solution, and no simple resolution.

Ironically, then, but revealingly, the first published version of Brown's story is presented in another's voice, that of Charles Stearns, who wrote *Narrative of Henry Box Brown, Who Escaped from Slavery Enclosed in a Box 3 Feet Long and 2 Wide. Written from a Statement of Facts Made by Himself. With Remarks Upon the Remedy for Slavery*. While Stearns acknowledges his role as author, he presents this 1849 *Narrative* not as a biography, with Stearns reporting what he has learned of Brown's life by talking with Brown, but rather as an autobiography, with Stearns writing at times for himself and at times for Brown. This was not unusual, for other slave narratives were written by someone to whom the main subject of the narrative, the former slave, dictated her or his story. Indeed, some of the most famous narratives of their time were written in this way, by an amanuensis—among them those of Solomon Northup and Josiah Henson. Henson became known as the model for Harriet Beecher Stowe's character Tom in *Uncle Tom's Cabin* (making Henson at least twice removed from his own story). Stearns, though, is very visibly a presence in the story, and his voice is rarely believable as an approximation of Brown's. Moreover, Stearns both prepares for and follows his presentation of Brown's supposedly autobiographical account with religious and political "remarks upon the remedy for slavery,"[48] making very clear Stearns's views on the importance and implications of this story, and on what should follow from it.[49]

To be sure, Stearns brought uncompromising passion to Brown's story. Stearns was, Jeffrey Ruggles rightly notes, an "unusual man," "very individual" in both his beliefs and his "radical" commitment to social reform.[50] His Christianity, Ruggles observes, "drew on the ecstatic meetings of the [revival] tents and was molded by his pacifism and abolitionism. He was probably influenced as well by the writings of his uncle George Ripley and the other Transcendentalists who emerged in the 1830s."[51] In his essay "Cure for the Evil of Slavery," which concludes the narrative of Brown's escape, Stearns condemns the corruption of Christianity in the United States.[52] "Our God," Stearns declares, "is emphatically Slavery. To him we address our early matins, and in his ear are uttered our evening orisons. More devoutly do we render homage to our god, Slavery, than the most pious of us adore the God of heaven, which proves that we are a very religious people, worshipping, not crocodiles, leeks and onions, snakes, and images of wood and stone, but a god, whose service is infinitely more disgusting than that of any heathen idol, but one who *pays* us well, for our obeisance, as we imagine."[53] Not surprisingly, then, long before his partnership with Brown, Stearns had been publicly critical of more moderate approaches to Christianity that were not sternly opposed to slavery, war, and alcohol, and he had suggested that "there is so much bad" in the Bible that "in its present form, I doubt its utility to the world."[54] Having established himself as a printer in Boston by 1847, and having published various antislavery and political tracts, Stearns was prepared to be of great service to Brown, and the narrative that they produced together during the summer of 1849 appeared in September with "Brown & Stearns" listed as the publishers.[55]

Readers of Stearns's narrative will learn a great deal about Brown's life, but they will learn a great deal more about Stearns's views on slavery, government, and religion in America. In "Cure for the Evil of Slavery," Stearns argues against the authority of the nation's "cannibal laws" and calls for "the immediate formation of *a new government at the North*."[56] In the essay, Stearns speaks in his own voice; but in the narrative, he speaks for Brown, and so Stearns uses his role as Brown to introduce his own essay, thus indicating the dynamics that define his role-playing throughout the narrative. "I do not understand much about laws, to be sure," Stearns has Brown say, "as the law of my master is the one I have been subject to all my life, but some how, it looks a little singular to me, that wise people should be obliged to break their own laws, or else do a very wicked act." Noting the need for one prepared to address the subject adequately, Stearns's Brown then introduces Stearns: "I now wish to introduce to your hearing a friend of mine, who will tell you more about these things than I can, until I have had more time to examine this curious subject."[57] Throughout the narrative, Stearns has Brown set the stage for his own ongoing commentary on the evils of slavery and the necessity of a new government, and one can only wonder how well Brown's interests are represented by either the commentary or the envisioned government.

After Brown managed his second escape from slavery—this time from the insecurities enforced by the Fugitive Slave Act of 1850—he published a second version of his narrative, *Narrative of the Life of Henry Box Brown, Written by Himself*. But the authorship of Brown's second narrative (what he called the "First English Edition") remains a complex affair. Although scholar Richard Newman suggests that preparing the 1851 version was a matter of editing "Stearns' overblown rhetoric [in the 1849 version] out of the narrative,"[58] Stearns's narration in fact remains a guiding presence in the 1851 *Narrative*, and as Brown's most recent biographer Jeffrey Ruggles notes, the familiar phrase "written by himself" in the title of this version of Brown's story is deceptive. "Although the 1851 *Narrative* is more directly Brown's expression than the 1849 *Narrative*," Ruggles asserts, "Brown did not put the words on paper."[59] Ruggles notes that "the new edition stays closer to the story, and it is clearer that Brown was the original source," but he notes as well that "the writer of the 1851 *Narrative* remains unidentified."[60] What we can know is that the differences between the 1849 and the 1851 versions of Brown's narrative are considerable, and that the Henry Box Brown whom we encounter in the 1851 *Narrative* does not prepare the stage for anyone beyond Henry Box Brown himself, whose public performances are built into the narrative.

While the 1849 version is important, the 1851 version is generally accepted as the fullest and most faithful representation of Brown's own account of his life. To be sure, traces of Stearns's rhetoric remain—significant words, phrases, and sentences are retained and rearranged throughout the narrative, though usually displayed in less elaborate settings.[61] Other voices are present in the 1851 version as well. Following a preface attributed to Brown, for example, is an introduction by the Reverend Thomas Gardiner Lee of Salford, England, which in addition to standard British antislavery rhetoric ("the roar of the British Lion") includes testimonials from a number of individuals, including antislavery activists James Miller McKim and Samuel J. May, along with various individuals who had seen Brown's panorama. Quoted lines from poetry, presented in the original narrative, reappear in 1851, though sometimes augmented (as with the lines from Bernard Barton's "A Child's Dream" in chapter 1), and new verses appear (for example, the lines gathered from James Merrick's *The Psalms* and from Isaac Watts's "Hymn 99" that close chapter 2). The white Baptist evangelist Elder Jacob Knapp, from New York state, not mentioned in 1849, makes an important appearance in 1851, along with the text (from Matthew 23:37) for his sermon in Richmond. There, too, is the less encouraging Reverend Robert

Ryland of Virginia, to whom "the coloured people had to pay . . . a salary of 700 dollars per annum, although they neither chose him nor had the least control over him." Church hymns, absent in 1849, are quoted in 1851. The 1851 version, in short, directs the reader to various people, texts, and events not mentioned in 1849 and in this way contextualizes Brown's life more complexly than does the 1849 version.

Most of this information could only have come from Brown himself. Names and dates that only Brown could provide, as well as specific experiences, are included in the 1851 narrative, along with more detailed notice of significant encounters and local sites—for example, the First African Baptist Church of Richmond that Brown had attended. And the narrative includes as well not only the songs that Brown performed in his public appearances but also other performance pieces for which he had become known. Indeed, by the time this narrative was produced, Brown had gained experience as a lecturer; he had collaborated with others to create and tour with his panorama, and he had become a presence in the U.S. and British presses. Even before the publication of his first narrative, Brown himself had distributed two song sheets, both associated with his escape, and he had distributed as well a lithograph of the *Resurrection of Henry Box Brown, at Philadelphia*, an image that was adapted for the frontispiece illustration of the 1851 *Narrative*. In short, the 1851 narrative represents not only the Henry Brown who escaped from slavery but also Henry "Box" Brown, the emerging antislavery celebrity.

Indeed, those who had witnessed Brown's public appearances would have recognized much of the material included in the 1851 narrative. The 1849 *Narrative* featured at the beginning the lyrics to the "Hymn of Thanksgiving" that Brown was said to have sung upon his emergence from the shipping crate in Philadelphia. These lyrics (or, rather, the verses from Psalm 40, on which Brown's song was based) were first printed as a song sheet, which included an image of a sealed crate marked for shipment to Philadelphia, that Brown made available to audiences at his antislavery appearances. Brown sang this hymn at those performances, and he sang as well a song describing his escape, with the lyrics set to the tune of Stephen Foster's blackface minstrel composition "Old Uncle Ned," a song also printed as a song sheet, with the same image of the shipping crate, for distribution at his performances. The 1849 narrative includes, immediately following Stearns's preface, the "Hymn of Thanksgiving" but not Brown's reworking of "Uncle Ned." In the 1851 narrative, both songs are included, and in close proximity—the hymn at the narrative moment when Brown emerges from the box, and the minstrel tune, which closes the narrative proper, a paragraph later. The connecting paragraph quickly takes Brown from his arrival in Philadelphia to his increasing involvement in and public appearances for the antislavery movement. The 1851 narrative includes as well Brown's story about "the shovel and the hoe," adapted from Foster's song, a story Brown almost certainly related on the stage.

As the more detailed account indicates, the 1851 *Narrative* provided Brown with the forum he needed to relate not simply the facts but the heart of his story. In successive chapters of the *Narrative*, containing material largely absent from the 1849 publication, the reader is introduced to Brown's account of his religious conversion—that is, his conversion to an understanding of religion in defiance of what he calls "the pretended Christianity under which I was trained, while a slave"—and this is the story that provides the important connection between the loss of his family and his successful escape. The relatively brief fifth chapter addresses "the state of churches in slave countries," focusing on the hypocrisies of slaveholding religion but including an account of the white northern evangelist and opponent of slavery Jacob Knapp, who once visited and preached in Richmond. The following chapter, the longest in the *Narrative*, takes the reader from Brown's decision to marry to the scene where Brown watches first his child and then his wife carried away in chains to another owner, never to be seen by him again. Brown had seen slave coffles before, but the sight of his child and his wife being taken away "made it assume the appearance of unusual horror"—indeed, a hellish vision of "little children of many different families, which as they appeared rent the air with their shrieks and cries and vain endeavours to resist the separation which was thus forced upon them, and the cords with which they were thus bound." This is followed by Brown's final chapter, including his account of his escape. In these chapters, Brown moves from situation to consequence to strategy—that is, from an account of a culture of corrupt Christianity to an account of the trauma that necessarily follows from that corruption and then to an account of the faith for which his traumatic experience prepared him. Brown's successful escape is the product of the entire process, and the story of his escape should include an understanding of the great loss he had suffered and the painful strength he had discovered through his suffering.

The chapters come to a point not when Brown is inspired to enter a box but, rather, when he is inspired to resist the box he is in, the moral hell of slavery. The final chapter of the *Narrative* begins with Brown's disavowal of religion and the specific occasion of his return to the church. "The suspicion of these slave-dealing christians," Brown reports, "was the means of keeping me absent from all their churches from the time that my wife and children were torn from me, until Christmas day in the year 1848; and I would not have gone then but being a leading member of the choir, I yielded to the entreaties of my associates to assist at a concert of sacred music which was to be got up for the benefit of the church." During the performance, one of Brown's fellow choir members, James C. A. Smith, suddenly closed his book and sat down. "Dr. Smith's feelings," Brown reports in the 1851 *Narrative*, "were overcome with a sense of doing wrongly in singing for the purpose of obtaining money to assist those who were buying and selling their fellow-men. He thought at that moment he felt reproved by Almighty God for lending his aid to the cause of slave-holding religion." After "several other pieces" Brown sings lines that have a similar effect on him: "Vital spark of heavenly flame, / Quit, O! quit the mortal frame." What gives the lines particular significance, Brown states, is "the sting of former sufferings," the loss of his wife and child, and Brown accordingly follows Smith's example: "I too made up my mind that I would be no longer guilty of assisting those bloody dealers in the bodies and souls of men." The experience leads to Brown's resolution to escape and, eventually, his successful plan when the idea of a box comes to him following a "prayer to Almighty God."

In this narrative, Brown extends his moral responsibilities to the antislavery cause, and his narrative is a reminder that an escape from slavery was rarely an occasion for an unqualified celebration. The *Narrative of the Life of Henry Box Brown, Written by Himself*, like other so-called slave narratives, is a complex meditation on the instabilities of the world created by the nation's reliance on the system of slavery and its devotion to the fictions of race. Like many other fugitive slaves, in writing for a British readership, Brown hoped to find an audience for his story that would add international force to the antislavery movement in the United States. More than that, though, Brown looked for a proper telling of his story, an account of his life that would not violate the many lives left behind in the American South. And he looked as well for a place for himself in a world that was ruled, in England as well as in his home country, by the priorities of white supremacist laws and prejudices.

It remains an open question as to whether Brown ever found either his audience or his home. He was never reunited with his wife and children, and by the end of the 1850s he had taken a second wife in England.[62] Brown continued to make public appearances throughout the 1850s. By 1852, he had added new features to his panorama and new songs to his performance, now exhibited under the title *Panorama of African and American Slavery*, and he dressed and billed himself as an "African Prince." At the end of the decade, he traveled with his wife and two panoramas, one titled the *Grand Original Panorama of African and American Slavery* and the other devoted to the resistance to British colonial rule in India. Shortly after, Brown began to include in his performances "several experiments in mesmerism, human magnetism, and electro-biology."[63] By 1862, responding to the Civil War in the United States, Brown's public appearances included new panoramas, the *Original Mirror of Africa and America* and the *Grand Moving Mirror of the American War*. By 1864, Brown was billing himself as the "King of all Mesmerisers" and exhibiting his *Panorama of African and American Slavery*. His public performances continued until 1875, when he finally returned to the United States with his wife and their daughter. Now sixty years old, Brown performed as a magician, billing himself as Prof. H. Box Brown. He still included in his advertisements the dimensions of the box in which he escaped.

Henry Box Brown's varied career indicates the complexity of life waiting at the other end of the many celebrated escapes from slavery that found their way into the antislavery press. Some of those who escaped from slavery turned to lecturing tours, and some to spiritualism. Some became ministers, and some became doctors; some became statesmen, and many others have been lost to the public record. The *Narrative of the Life of Henry Box Brown, Written by Himself* was not, of course, an attempt to capture the complexity of the nominal and restricted freedom awaiting those who escaped from slavery, nor is it a narrative capable of representing those many who remained in slavery, those whose lives have yet to find a proper narrative. Suffice it to say that this is both something more and something less than a narrative of escape, and that Brown's story deserves something more than fascination and celebration, even these many years after it was originally presented on the public stage. This remains a narrative in search of an audience, and a narrative with something to say even to today's readers.

Notes

1. Martineau, *Retrospect of Western Travel*, 251.

2. Douglass, *Narrative*, 85.

3. Douglass, *My Bondage and My Freedom*, 339.

4. On Brown's fame in the nineteenth century, see Ruggles, *Unboxing*, 151–52, 161–62. On Brown's regular appearances in twentieth- and twenty-first-century television programs, operas, musicals, plays, books, and museums, see ibid., 170–73. For virtually all biographical information on Henry Box Brown, I am greatly indebted to Ruggles's exemplary research.

5. See "Passenger in the Boot," 158.

6. The best overview of Brown's presence in scholarship and popular

culture is in Ruggles, *Unboxing*, 170–72. Concerning film, opera, and performance pieces, Ruggles states,

> In recent years, artists in a variety of mediums have found material in Brown's story. Patricia Khayyam's nine-minute film entitled "Henry Box Brown" (1990) has been shown at international film festivals. In the opera *Vanqui* by John A. Williams and Leslie Burrs, given its premiere in 1999 by Opera/Columbus in Ohio, the spirits of Vance and Prince encounter famous black freedom fighters, one of them Henry Box Brown. The Delaware Humanities Forum commissioned a musical, *Delaware's Railroad to Freedom*, in which Brown is a character; playwright and actor Mike Wiley centers his one-man performance piece, *One Noble Journey*, on Brown's escape; and Tony Kushner, author of the prizewinning drama *Angels in America*, has promised a new play entitled *Henry Box Brown, or, The Mirror of Slavery*. Brown has also inspired poems by Elizabeth Alexander, Lamont Steptoe, and A. Van Jordan. Artist Glenn Ligon's sculptural assemblage *To Disembark* includes marked wooden crates that refer to Henry Box Brown. Regarding her 1987 work, "32 Hours in a Box . . . Still Counting," artist Pat Ward Williams stated, "I think as black people we have to find different solutions to overcome the obstacles that are in our lives politically and also personally. This is a piece about Henry Box Brown and problem solving." (172)

For important studies of Brown's written work and public performances, see Brooks, *Bodies in Dissent*, 66–130; Fisch, *American Slaves*, 73–83; Grover, *Fugitive's Gibraltar*, 199–204; Wolff, "Passing Beyond the Middle Passage"; and Wood, *Blind Memory*, 103–17.

7. Still, *Underground Rail Road*, 67.

8. Ibid., 28, 634.

9. Ibid., 66.

10. Ibid., 38, 96.

11. For an account of this event, see Ruggles, *Unboxing*, 48–50.

12. Ibid., 56.

13. For the best background on and accounts of Brown's panorama, see ibid., 69–109, and Wolff, "Passing Beyond the Middle Passage." On the reception of Brown's panorama in England, see also Fisch, *American Slaves*, 74–83.

14. Quoted in Fisch, *American Slaves*, 73.

15. Hartman, *Scenes of Subjection*, 42.

16. Newspaper accounts of Brown's escape, or of his narrative, regularly emphasized his separation from his wife and children. Representative in this way and others is the account titled "Henry Box Brown," published originally in the *Boston Republican* and reprinted in the *Farmer's Cabinet*, which reports that, at an antislavery meeting, Brown "remarked, with the deepest pathos, that after his wife and children were stolen, his heart was broken. He had learned to sing to lighten the tedium of his labor, and for the gratification of his fellow-captives, but now he could not sing. His thoughts were far away in the rice swamps of Carolina or the cotton plantations of Georgia. His wife was not and his children were not, and he refused to be comforted" (1). See also Barker's response to this account, a poem titled "The Fugitive's Wife." Both pieces are included in Appendix B, "Henry Box Brown in the Press."

17. The church Brown attended was the First African Baptist Church of Richmond, Virginia. The Reverend Robert Ryland, a white minister, was president of Richmond College and pastor of Brown's church, which did not have a black pastor until James Henry Holmes, a longtime deacon of the church, replaced Ryland in 1866. The First African Baptist Church was formed in 1841, drawing its membership from the First Baptist Church of Richmond, in which black members had long outnumbered white members. The church had more than 2,000 members in 1843 and over 3,000 in 1860. For background and commentary on the First African Baptist Church, more generous to both the church and Ryland than that presented here, see Billingsley, *Mighty Like a River*, 62–84.

18. Price and Stewart, "Introduction," 6.

19. Violence against those involved in the antislavery movement was quite frequent. In 1970, Leonard L. Richards began his important study of anti-abolition mobs in the Jacksonian era with a useful overview and an important question:

> For over a century historians have been telling us that Northerners
> dragged the antislavery agitator William Lloyd Garrison through the
> streets of Boston in 1835; broke up a convention of the New York State
> Anti-Slavery Society at Utica on the same day; petitioned in 1835 and
> 1836 for legislation to make the propagation of abolitionist senti-

ments a criminal offense; supplied the necessary votes to pass the famous gag rule which was renewed at each session of Congress between 1836 and 1844; established the Connecticut gag law in 1836 to bar abolitionist lecturers from Congregational pulpits; murdered the abolitionist editor Elijah Lovejoy at Alton, Illinois, in 1837; burned down Pennsylvania Hall in Philadelphia in 1838. But why? (*"Gentlemen of Property and Standing,"* 3)

Richards rightly suggests that "it no longer seems possible for historians to dismiss these happenings as simply aberrations in an otherwise healthy and enlightened society" (ibid., 3). For a particularly thorough and instructive study of this violence, see Grimsted, *American Mobbing*.

20. Garnet, "Address to the Slaves," 283.

21. The evidence suggests that Walker probably died of consumption. See Hinks, *To Awaken My Afflicted Brethren*, 269–71. Hinks adds that "certainly there were numerous Southerners who wanted Walker dead, and neither the possibility of murder nor the possibility that he was stalked can be discounted" (269–70).

22. For a good introduction to the cases mentioned here and beyond, see Campbell, *Slave Catchers*.

23. The material on John Brown and Nat Turner appeared in the last issue of the first volume of the *Anglo-African Magazine* (1859). A bound edition of that volume was published in that same year, thus emphasizing this material at the culmination of the year's publications. For a discussion of this volume, see Ernest, *Liberation Historiography*, 305–29.

24. Gilroy, *Black Atlantic*, 4.

25. Ripley, introduction, 6.

26. Ibid., 3.

27. Fisch, *American Slaves*, 4–5.

28. Carey, *British Abolitionism*, 2.

29. Ibid.

30. Lee, *Slavery and the Romantic Imagination*, 6.

31. McBride, *Impossible Witnesses*, 17.

32. Ibid., 18.

33. Ibid., 4.

34. Litwack, "Emancipation of the Negro Abolitionist," 115.

35. Pease and Pease, "Antislavery Ambivalence," 97–98. Parker's letter

was published as *John Brown's Expedition Reviewed in a Letter from Theodore Parker, at Rome, to Francis Jackson, Boston* (Boston, 1860); the Peases take the quotation from page 14 of that pamphlet.

36. Lorimer, *Colour, Class and the Victorians*, 54.

37. "Reception," 166.

38. "Celebration," 139.

39. Douglass, "Self-Elevation," 360-61.

40. Douglass, "Unholy Alliance," 387.

41. For more on white supremacy as a presence in the antislavery movement, and a dynamic in the presentation and reception of the stories of the formerly enslaved, see Ernest, *Liberation Historiography*, 163-210.

42. On the incidents in New Hampshire and Connecticut, see Litwack, *North of Slavery*, 117-20, 126-31.

43. Brown, *Lecture Delivered Before the Female Anti-Slavery Society of Salem*, 4.

44. For background on slave narratives, and on the cultural politics influencing the composition and the reception of the narratives, see Andrews, *To Tell a Free Story*; Braxton, *Black Women Writing Autobiography*; Davis and Gates, *Slave's Narrative*; Fisch, *Cambridge Companion to the African American Slave Narrative*; Foster, *Witnessing Slavery*; Rohrbach, *Truth Stranger Than Fiction*, 29-50; and Starling, *Slave Narrative*.

45. Peabody, "Narratives of Fugitive Slaves," 19. For a balanced account of this important article, see Andrews, *To Tell a Free Story*, 97-99. For a discussion of the influence of Peabody's article on Harriet Beecher Stowe, author of *Uncle Tom's Cabin*, see Starling, *Slave Narrative*, 297-306.

46. Bibb, *Life and Adventures of Henry Bibb*, 1.

47. Hartman, *Scenes of Subjection*, 42.

48. Stearns, *Narrative of Henry Box Brown*, iii.

49. For a sampling of Stearns's handling of the *Narrative*, see Appendix C, "From the United States to England: The Two Narratives."

50. Ruggles, *Unboxing*, 59, 60.

51. Ibid., 60.

52. Stearns, *Narrative of Henry Box Brown*, 67.

53. Ibid., 81-82.

54. Ibid., 61.

55. Stearns was singular in many respects, but his strong views were not entirely unusual among white abolitionists. As Gienapp has observed in his general overview of white antislavery activists,

> While they were often successful in their careers and were not a displaced social elite, they were nevertheless deeply alienated from American society. They deplored the lack of religion in American life, the rampant materialism, and the crassness and pragmatism of American politics. They were shocked by the failure of the campaign in the 1820s to stop the movement of the U.S. mails on the Sabbath. By the 1830s their vague discontent began to come into sharp focus, as they concluded that slavery was the fundamental cause of the nation's degradation. Abolitionism became the means to save the country. ("Abolitionism and the Nature of Antebellum Reform," 32–33)

The most famous and influential white abolitionist, William Lloyd Garrison, exemplified this alienation. "Strongly influenced by John Humphrey Noyes's radical brand of Christian perfectionism," Gienapp notes, "Garrison endorsed a number of radical ideas, which constituted his 'broad program' of reform" (ibid., 35–36).

56. Stearns, *Narrative of Henry Box Brown*, 71, 67.

57. Ibid., 65–66.

58. Newman, introduction, xii.

59. Ruggles, *Unboxing*, 129.

60. Ibid., 129, 132. Newman, who wrote the introduction for the first U.S. publication of the 1851 *Narrative* in 2002, observes that "unable to read or write and with little access to printers or publishers, Box Brown was not free from saying what other people wanted him to say. Only in England did he experience the freedom to express himself in his own way. The Manchester edition is obviously closer to Brown's own telling of his own story" (introduction, xii).

61. Interestingly, the spelling of some words changes from one version to the next; for example, "endeavored" in 1849 becomes "endeavoured" in 1851, suggesting either a "correction" by the British printer or that Brown might have received assistance from a British writer.

62. Ruggles reports that Brown's second wife "was almost certainly English, but of her, and of their marriage, there is no information except from reports of the shows. Because advertisements and articles identify

her only as 'Mrs. H. Box Brown,' not even her given name is known. Several accounts describe her performances as accomplished, an indication that she probably had a background in show business prior to their marriage" (*Unboxing*, 152).

63. Quoted in ibid., 154.

A NOTE ON THE TEXT

The *Narrative of the Life of Henry Box Brown* presented here is based on the "First English Edition," printed by Lee and Glynn in Manchester, England, in 1851. I am grateful to the Albert H. Small Special Collections Library of the University of Virginia for making this book available to me.

Obvious spelling or printing errors have been corrected, but otherwise the original spellings have been retained to capture the sometimes suggestive details of the original and to preserve the British flavor of the text published in England.

RESURRECTION OF HENRY BOX BROWN, AT PHILADELPHIA.

Resurrection of Henry Box Brown, at Philadelphia.
Frontispiece from *Narrative of the Life of Henry Box Brown, Written by Himself.*
Manchester: Lee and Glynn, 1851. Engraving by Langton.
Courtesy of Special Collections, University of Virginia Library.

NARRATIVE
of the
LIFE OF HENRY BOX BROWN,
WRITTEN BY HIMSELF.
FIRST ENGLISH EDITION.

Forget not the unhappy,
Though sorrow may annoy,
There's something then for memory,
Hereafter to enjoy!
Oh! still from Fortune's garland,
Some flowers for others strew;
And forget not the unhappy,
*For, ah! their friends are few.*1

⊰ PREFACE ⊱

So much has already been written concerning the evils of slavery, and by men so much more able to portray its horrid form than I am, that I might well be excused if I were to remain altogether silent on the subject; but however much has been written, however much has been said, and however much has been done, I feel impelled by the voice of my own conscience, from the recent experience which I have had of the alarming extent to which the traffic in human beings is carried on, and the cruelties, both bodily and mental, to which men in the condition of slaves are continually subjected, and also from the hardening and blasting influences which this traffic produces on the character of those who thus treat as goods and chattels the bodies and souls of their fellows, to add yet one other testimony of, and protest against, the foul blot on the state of morals, of religion, and of cultivation in the American republic. For I feel convinced that enough has not been written, enough has not been said, enough has not been done, while nearly four millions of human beings, possessing immortal souls, are, in chains, dragging out their existence in the southern states. They are keenly alive to the heaven born voice of liberty, and require the illumination of the grace of Almighty God. Having, myself, been in that same position, but by the blessing of God having been enabled to snap my chains and escape to a land of liberty—I owe it as a sacred duty to the cause of humanity, that I should devote my life to the redemption of my fellow men.

The tale of my own sufferings is not one of great interest to those who delight to read of hair-breadth adventures, of tragical occurrences, and scenes of blood:—my life, even in slavery, has been in many respects comparatively comfortable. I have experienced a continuance of such kindness, as slaveholders have to bestow; but though my body has escaped the lash of the whip, my mind has groaned under tortures which I believe will never be related, because, language is inadequate to express them, but those know them who have them to endure. The whip, the cowskin, the gallows, the stocks, the paddle, the prison, the perversion of the stomach—although bloody and barbarous in their nature—have no comparison with those internal pangs which are felt by the soul when the hand of the merciless tyrant plucks from one's bosom the object of one's ripened affections, and the darlings who in requiring parental care, confer the sweet sensations of parental bliss. I freely admit I have enjoyed my full share of all those blessings which fall to the lot of a slave's existence. I have felt the sweet influence of friendship's power, and the still more delightful glow of love; and had I never heard the name of liberty or seen the tyrant lift his cruel hand to smite my fellow and my friend, I might perhaps have dragged my chains in quietude to the grave, and have found a tomb in a slavery-polluted land; but thanks be to God I heard the glorious sound and felt its inspiring influence on my heart, and having satisfied myself of the value of freedom I resolved to purchase it whatever should be its price.

While America is boasting of her freedom and making the world ring with her professions of equality, she holds millions of her inhabitants in bondage. This surely must be a wonder to all who seriously reflect on the subject of man holding property in man, in a land of republican institutions. That slavery, in all its phases, is demoralizing to every one concerned, none who may read the following narrative, can for a moment doubt. In my opinion unless the Americans purge themselves of this stain, they will have to undergo very severe, if not protracted suffering. It is not at all unlikely that the great unsettledness which of late has attached to the prices of cotton; the very unsatisfactory circumstance of that slaveholding continent being the principal field employed in the production of that vegetable, by the dealing in, and the manufacture of, which, such astonishing fortunes have been amassed — will lead to arrangements being entered into, through the operation of which the bondmen will be made free. The popular mind is, in every land becoming impatient of its chains; and soon the American captives will be made to taste of that freedom, which by right, belongs to man. The manner in which this mighty change will be accomplished, may not be at present understood, but with the Lord all things are possible. It may be, that the very means which are being used by those who wish to perpetuate slavery, and to recapture those who have by any plans not approved of by those dealers in human flesh, become free, will be amongst the instruments which God will employ to overturn the whole system.

Another means which, in addition to the above, we think, will contribute to the accomplishment of this desirable object — the destruction of slavery — is the simple, but natural narrations of those who have been long under the yoke themselves. It is a lamentable fact that some ministers of religion are contaminated with the foulness of slavery. Those men, in the southern states, who ascend the pulpit to proclaim the world's jubilee, are themselves, in fearful numbers, the holders of slaves! When we reflect on the bar which slavery constituted to the advancement of the objects at one time contemplated by the almost defunct "Evangelical Alliance";[2]

when we consider that Great Being who beheld the Israelites in their captivity, and beholding, came down to deliver them is still the same; have we not reason to believe that he will in his Providence raise up another Moses,[3] to guide the now enslaved sons of Ham[4] to the privileges which humanity, irrespective of colour or clime, is always at liberty to demand. While the British mind retain its antipathy to slavery in all its kinds, and send forth its waves of audibly expressed opinion on the subject, that opinion; meeting with one nearly allied in character to itself in the Northern States; and while both unite in tending towards the South the reiterated demand for an honest acting, one whose turgid profession of equality peculiar to all American proceedings—in every thing but slavery—the Southern states must yield to the pressure from without; even the slaves will feel themselves growing beyond the dimensions which their chains can enclose, and backed by the roar of the British Lion, and supported by Northern Americans in their just demand for emancipation, the long downtrodden and despised bondmen will arise; and by a united voice assert their title to freedom. It may be that the subject of the following narrative has a mission from God to the human family. Certainly the deliverance of Moses, from destruction on the Nile, was scarcely more marvelous than was the deliverance of Mr. Henry Box Brown from the horrors of slavery. For any lengthy observations, by which the reader will be detained from the subject of the following pages, there can be no necessity whatever.

Mr. Brown was conveyed from Richmond, Virginia, to Philadelphia in a box, three feet long, and two feet six inches deep. For twenty-seven hours he was enclosed in this box. The following copy of a letter which was written by the gentleman to whom it was directed; will explain this part of the subject:—

Copy of a Letter respecting Henry Box Brown's escape from Slavery—a verification of Patrick Henry's Speech in Virginia Legislature, March, 1775, when he said, *"Give me Liberty or give me Death."*[5]

Philadelphia, March 26th, 1849.

DEAR——[6]

Here is a man who has been the hero of one of the most extraordinary achievements I ever heard of;—he came to me on Saturday Morning last, in a box tightly hooped, marked "THIS SIDE UP," by *overland express, from the city of Richmond!!* Did you ever hear of any thing in all your life to beat that? Nothing that was done on the barricades of Paris exceeded this cool and deliberate intrepidity. To appreciate fully the boldness and risk of the achievement, you ought to see the box and hear all the circumstances. The box is in the clear three feet one inch long, two feet six inches deep, and two feet wide. It was a regular old store box such as you see in Pearl-street;—it was grooved at the joints and braced at the ends, leaving but the very slightest crevice to admit the air. Nothing saved him from suffocation but the free use of water—a quantity of which he took in with him in a beef's bladder, and with which he bathed his face—and the constant fanning of himself with his hat. He fanned himself unremittingly all the time. The "this side up" on the box was not regarded, and he was twice put with his head downward, resting with his back against the end of the box, his feet braced against the other,—the first time he succeeded in shifting his position; but the second time was on board of the steam boat, where people were sitting and standing about the box, and where any motions inside would have been overheard and have led to discovery; he was therefore obliged to keep his position *for twenty miles*. This nearly killed him. He says the veins in his temples were as thick as his finger. I had been expecting him for several days, and was in mortal fear all the time lest his arrival should only be a signal for calling in the coroner. You can better imagine than I can describe my sensations, when, in answer to my rap on the box and question, "*all right,*" the prompt response came "all right, sir." The man weighs 200 pounds, and is about five feet eight inches in height; and is, as you will see, a noble looking fellow. He will tell you the whole story. Please send him on to Mr. Mc-Gleveland, Boston, with this letter, to save me the time it would take to write another. He was boxed up in Richmond, at five, A.M. on Friday shipped at eight, and I opened him up at six (about daylight) next morning. He has a sister in New Bedford.

Yours, truly,

M. MCROY.[7]

The report of Mr. Brown's escape spread far and wide, so that he was introduced to the Anti-Slavery Society in Philadelphia, from the office of which society a letter, of which the following is a copy, was written.

Anti-Slavery Office,
Philadelphia, April 8th, 1850.

H. BOX BROWN,

MY DEAR SIR,—I was pleased to learn, by your letter, that it was your purpose to publish a narrative of the circumstances of your escape from slavery; such a publication, I should think, would not only be highly interesting, but well adapted to help on the cause of anti-slavery. Facts of this kind illustrate, without comment, the cruelty of the slave system, the fitness of its victims for freedom, and, at the same time, the guilt of the nation that tolerates its existence.

As one privy to many of the circumstances of your escape, I consider it one of the most remarkable exploits on record. That a man should come all the way from Richmond to Philadelphia, by the overland route, packed up in a box three feet long, by two and an half feet wide and deep, with scarcely a perceptible crevice for the admission of fresh air, and subject, at that time, to the rough handling and frequent shiftings of other freight, and that he should reach his destination alive, is a tale scarcely to be believed on the most irresistible testimony. I confess, if I had not myself been present at the opening of the box on its arrival, and had not witnessed with my own eyes, your resurrection from your living tomb, I should have been strongly disposed to question the truth of the story. As it was, however, seeing was believing, and believing was with me, at least, to be impressed with the diabolical character of American Slavery, and the obligation that rests upon every one to labour for its overthrow.

Trusting that this may be the impression produced by your narrative, wherever it is read, and that it may be read wherever the evils of slavery are felt, I remain,

Your friend truly,

J. MCKIM.

Were Mr. Brown in quest of an apology for publishing the following Narrative the letter of Mr. Mc Kim would form that apology. The Narrative was published in America, and an edition of 8,000 copies sold in about two months, such was the interest excited by the astounding revelations made by Mr. Brown as to the real character of slavery, and the hypocrisy of those professors of religion who have any connection with its infernal proceedings.[8]

Several ministers of religion took a great interest in Mr. Brown, and did what they could to bring the subject of his escape properly before the public. The Rev. Mr. Spauldin, of Dover, N.H. was at the trouble to write to two of his brethren in the ministry, a letter, of which the following is a copy. The testimonials subjoining Mr. Spauldin's letter were given by persons who had witnessed the exhibition.

TO THE REV. MESSRS. PIKE AND BROOKS.

Dover, 12th July, 1850

DEAR BRETHREN,

A coloured gentleman, Mr. H. B. Brown, purposes to visit your village for the purpose of exhibiting his splendid PANORAMA, or MIRROR OF SLAVERY.[9] I have had the pleasure of seeing it, and am prepared to say, from what I have myself seen, and known in times past, of slavery and of the slave trade, in my opinion, it is almost, if not quite, a perfect *fac simile* of the workings of that horrible and fiendish system. The real *life-like* scenes presented in this PANORAMA, are admirably calculated to make an unfading impression upon the heart and memory, such as no lectures, books, or colloquial correspondence can produce, especially on the minds of children and young people, who should every where be brought before the altar of Hannibal, to swear eternal hate to slavery, and love of rational freedom. If you can spare the time to witness the exhibition, I am quite certain you will feel yourselves amply rewarded. I know very well, there are a great many impostors and cheats going about through the country deceiving and picking up the people's money, but *this* is of another class altogether.

Yours, very truly,

JUSTIN SPAULDING.[10]

I hereby certify that I have attended the exhibition of H. B. Brown's Panorama, in this village, with very deep interest; and most cordially subscribe my name, as an expression of my full concurrence with the sentiment of the recommendation above.

A. LATHAM.[11]

I agree cordially in the above testimonials.

A. CAVERNO.[12]

I am not an experienced judge in paintings of this kind; but am only surprised that this is so well done and so much of it true to the life.

OLIVER AYER PORRER.

Of Franklin-street, Baptist Minister.

Dover, N.H. July 15th, 1850.

Although the following letter, as to date, should have occupied a place before the others, as it was addressed to the public and not to any particular person, its present position will answer every purpose of its publication.

Syracuse, April 26th, 1850.

There are few facts, connected with the terrible history of American Slavery, that will be longer remembered, than that a man escaped from the house of bondage, by coming from Richmond, Virginia, to Philadelphia, in a box *three feet, one inch long, two feet wide, and two feet six inches deep.* Twenty-seven hours he was closely packed within those small dimensions, and was tumbled along on drays, railroad cars, steam-boat, and horse carts, as any other box of merchandize would have been, sometimes on his feet, sometimes on his side, and once, for an hour or two, actually on his head.

Such is the well attested fact, and this volume contains the biography of the remarkable man, Henry Box Brown, who thus attained his freedom. Is there a man in our country, who better deserves his liberty? And is there to be found in these northern states, an individual base enough to assist in returning him to slavery! or to stand quietly by and consent to his recapture?

The narrative of such a man cannot fail to be interesting, and I cordially commend it to all who love liberty and hate oppression.

SAMUEL J. MAY.[13]

After Mr. Brown's arrival in the Free States and the recovery of his health, in addition to the publishing of his Narrative he began to prepare the Panorama, which has been exhibited with such success both in America and in England.

January, 1851.

WE, the Teachers of St. John's Sunday School, Blackburn, having seen the exhibition in our School-room, called the "Panorama of American Slavery," feel it our duty to call upon all our christian brethren, who may have an opportunity, to go and witness this great mirror of slavery for themselves, feeling assured ourselves that it is calculated to leave a lasting impression upon the mind, and particularly that of the young.

We recommend it more especially on account of the exhibitor, Mr. Henry Box Brown, being himself a fugitive slave, and therefore able to give a true account of all the horrors of American Slavery, together with his own miraculous escape.

Signed,

John Francis,	John Alston,
John Parkinson,	George Fielding,
Henry Ainsworth,	Thomas Higham,
John Tomlinson,	Daniel Tomlinson,
Henry Wilkinson,	Benjamin Cliff,
John Hartley,	John Howcutt,
James Greaves,	James Holt,
John Roberts,	Mark Shaw,
Francis Broughton,	Christopher Higham.

Mr. Brown continued to travel in the United States until the Fugitive Slave Bill—which passed into law last year—rendered it necessary for him to seek an asylum on British ground. Such was the vigilance with which the search for victims was pursued, that Mr. Brown had to travel under an assumed name, and by the most secret means shift his panorama to prevent suspicion and capture.

THOMAS G. LEE,[14]

Minister of New Windsor Chapel, Salford.

April 8, 1851.

NARRATIVE

of the LIFE OF

HENRY BOX
BROWN.

⊰ CHAPTER I ⊱

I was born about forty-five miles from the city of Richmond, in
Louisa County, in the year 1815. I entered the world a slave—in the
midst of a country whose most honoured writings declare that all
men have a right to liberty—but had imprinted upon my body no
mark which could be made to signify that my destiny was to be that
of a bondman. Neither was there any angel stood by, at the hour
of my birth, to hand my body over, by the authority of heaven, to
be the property of a fellow-man; no, but I was a slave because my
countrymen had made it lawful, in utter contempt of the declared
will of heaven, for the strong to lay hold of the weak and to buy
and to sell them as marketable goods. Thus was I born a slave;
tyrants—remorseless, destitute of religion and every principle
of humanity—stood by the couch of my mother and as I entered
into the world, before I had done anything to forfeit my right to
liberty, and while my soul was yet undefiled by the commission
of actual sin, stretched forth their bloody arms and branded me
with the mark of bondage, and by such means I became their own
property. Yes, they robbed me of myself before I could know the
nature of their wicked arts, and ever afterwards—until I forcibly
wrenched myself from their hands—did they retain their stolen
property.

My father and mother of course, were then slaves, but both
of them are now enjoying such a measure of liberty, as the law
affords to those who have made recompense to the tyrant for the
right of property he holds in his fellow-man. It was not my fortune to be long under my mother's care; but I still possess a vivid

recollection of her affectionate oversight. Such lessons as the following she would frequently give me. She would take me upon her knee and, pointing to the forest trees which were then being stripped of their foliage by the winds of autumn, would say to me, my son, as yonder leaves are stripped from off the trees of the forest, so are the children of the slaves swept away from them by the hands of cruel tyrants; and her voice would tremble and she would seem almost choked with her deep emotion, while the tears would find their way down her saddened cheeks. On those occasions she fondly pressed me to her heaving bosom, as if to save me from so dreaded a calamity, or to feast on the enjoyments of maternal feeling while she yet retained possession of her child. I was then young, but I well recollect the sadness of her countenance, and the mournful sacredness of her words as they impressed themselves upon my youthful mind—never to be forgotten.

Mothers of the North! as you gaze upon the fair forms of your idolised little ones, just pause for a moment; how would you feel if you knew that at any time the will of a tyrant—who neither could nor would sympathise with your domestic feelings—might separate them for ever from your embrace, not to be laid in the silent grave "where the wicked cease from troubling and where the weary are at rest,"[15] but to live under the dominion of tyrants and avaricious men, whose cold hearts cannot sympathise with your feelings, but who will mock at any manifestation of tenderness, and scourge them to satisfy the cruelty of their own disposition; yet such is the condition of hundreds of thousands of mothers in the southern states of America.

My mother used to instruct me in the principles of morality, according to her own notion of what was good and pure; but I had no means of acquiring proper conception of religion in a state of slavery, where all those who professed to be followers of Jesus Christ evinced more of the disposition of demons than of men; and it is really a matter of wonder to me now, considering the character of my position that I did not imbibe a strong and lasting hatred of every thing pertaining to the religion of Christ. My lessons in morality were of the most simple kind. I was told not to steal, not to tell lies, and to behave myself in a becoming manner towards everybody. My mother, although a slave, took great delight in watching the result of her moral training in the character of my brother and myself, whilst—whether successful or unsuccessful in the formation of superior habits in us it is not for me to say—there were sown for her a blissful remembrance in the minds of her children, which will be cherished, both by the bond and the free, as long as life shall last.

As a specimen of the religious knowledge of the slave, I may here state what were my impressions in regard to my master; assuring the reader that I am not joking but stating what were the opinions of all the slaves' children on my master's plantation, so that some judgment may be formed of the care which was taken of our religious instruction. I really believed my old master was Almighty God, and that the young master was Jesus Christ! The reason of this error seems to have been that we were taught to believe thunder to be the voice of God, and when it was about to thunder my old master would approach us, if we were in the yard, and say, all you children run into the house now, for it is going to thunder; and after the thunder storm was over he would approach us smilingly and say, "what a fine shower we have had," and bidding us look at the flowers would observe how prettily they appeared; we children seeing this so frequently, could not avoid the idea that it was he that thundered and made the rain to fall, in order to make his flowers look beautiful, and I was nearly eight years of age before I got rid of this childish superstition. Our master was uncommonly kind, (for even a slaveholder may be kind) and as he moved about in his dignity he seemed like a god to us, but notwithstanding his kindness, although he knew very well what superstitious notions we formed of him, he never made the least attempt to correct our erroneous impression, but rather seemed pleased with the reverential feelings which we entertained towards him. All the young slaves called his son saviour, and the manner in which I was undeceived was as follows.—One Sabbath after preaching time my mother told my father of a woman who wished to join the church. She had told the preacher that she had been baptised by one of the slaves at night—a practice which is quite common. After they went from their work to the minister he asked her if she believed that our Saviour came into the world and had died for the sins of men? And she said "yes." I was listening anxiously to the conversation, and when my mother had finished, I asked her if my young master was not the saviour whom the woman said was dead? She said he was not, but it was our Saviour in heaven. I then asked her if there was a saviour there too; when she told me that young master was not our Saviour;—which astonished me very much. I then asked her if old master was not he? to which she replied he was not, and began to instruct me more fully in reference to the God of heaven. After this I believed there was a God who ruled the world, but I did not previously entertain the least idea of any such Being; and however dangerous my former notions were, they were not at all out of keeping with the blasphemous teachings of the hellish system of slavery.

One of my sisters became anxious to have her soul converted, and for this purpose had the hair cut from her head, because it is a notion which prevails amongst the slaves, that unless the hair be cut the soul cannot be converted. My mother reproved her for this and told her that she must pray to God who dwelled in heaven, and who only could convert her soul; and said if she wished to renounce the sins of the world she should recollect that it was not by outside show, such as the cutting of the hair, that God measured the worthi- or unworthiness of his servants. "Only ask of God," she said, "with an humble heart, forsaking your sins in obedience to his divine commandment, and whatever mercy is most fitting for your condition he will graciously bestow."

While quite a lad my principal employment was waiting upon my master and mistress, and at intervals taking lessons in the various kinds of work which was carried on on the plantation: and I have often, there—where the hot sun sent forth its scorching rays upon my tender head—looked forward with dismay to the time when I, like my fellow slaves, should be driven by the taskmaster's cruel lash, to separate myself from my parents and all my present associates, to toil without reward and to suffer cruelties, as yet unknown. The slave has always the harrowing idea before him—however kindly he may be treated for the time being—that the auctioneer may soon set him up for public sale and knock him down as the property of the person who, whether man or demon, would pay his master the greatest number of dollars for his body.

⊰ CHAPTER II ⊱

My brother and myself were in the habit of carrying grain to the mill a few times in the year, which was the means of furnishing us with some information respecting other slaves, otherwise we would have known nothing whatever of what was going on anywhere in the world, excepting on our master's plantation. The mill was situated at a distance of about 20 miles from our residence, and belonged to one Colonel Ambler, in Yansinville county. On these occasions we used to acquire some little knowledge of what was going on around us, and we neglected no opportunity of making ourselves acquainted with the condition of other slaves.

On one occasion, while waiting for grain, we entered a house in the neighbourhood, and while resting ourselves there, we saw a number of forlorn looking beings pass the door, and as they passed we noticed they gazed earnestly upon us; afterwards about fifty did the very same, and we heard some of them remarking that we had shoes, vests, and hats. We felt a desire to talk with them, and, accordingly after receiving some bread and meat from the mistress of the house we followed those abject beings to their quarters, and such a sight we had never witnessed before, as we had always lived on our master's plantation, and this was the first of our journeys to the mill. These Slaves were dressed in shirts made of coarse bagging such as coffee sacks are made from, and some kind of light substance for pantaloons, and this was all their clothing! They had no shoes, hats, vests, or coats, and when my brother spoke of their poor clothing they said they had never before seen colored persons dressed as we were; they looked very hungry, and we divided our bread and meat among them. They said they never had any meat given them by their master. My brother put various questions to them, such as if they had wives? did they go to church? &c., they said they had wives, but were obliged to marry persons who worked on the same plantation, as the master would not allow them to take wives from other plantations, consequently they were all related to each other, and the master obliged them to marry their relatives or to remain single. My brother asked one of them to show him his sisters:—he said he could not distinguish them from the rest, as they were all his sisters. Although the slaves themselves entertain considerable respect for the law of marriage as a moral principle, and are exceedingly well pleased when they can obtain the services of a minister in the performance of the ceremony, yet the law recognizes no right in slaves to marry at all. The relation of husband and wife, parent and child, only exists by the toleration of their master, who may insult the slave's wife, or violate her person at any moment, and there is no law to punish him for what he has done. Now this not only may be as I have said, but it actually is the case to an alarming extent; and it is my candid opinion, that one of the strongest motives which operate upon the slaveholders in inducing them to maintain their iron grasp upon the unfortunate slaves, is because it gives them such unlimited control over the person of their female slaves. The greater part of slaveholders are licentious men, and the most respectable and kind masters keep some of these slaves as mistresses. It is for their pecuniary interest to do so, as their progeny is equal to so many dollars and cents in their pockets, instead of being a source of expense to them, as would be the case, if their slaves were free. It is a horrible idea, but it is no less true, that no slave husband has any certainty whatever of being able to retain his wife a single hour; neither has any wife any more certainty of her husband; their fondest affection may be utterly disregarded, and their devoted attachment cruelly ignored at any moment a brutal slave-holder may think fit.

The slaves on Col. Ambler's plantation were never allowed to attend church, but were left to manage their religious affairs in their own way. An old slave whom they called John, decided on their religious profession and would baptize the approved parties during the silent watches of the night, while their master was asleep. We might have got information on many things from these slaves of Col. Ambler, but, while we were thus engaged, we perceived the overseer directing his steps towards us like a bear for its prey: we had however, time to ask one of them if they were ever whipped? to which he replied that not a day passed over their heads without some of them being brutally punished; "and," said he, "we shall have to suffer for this talk with you. It was but this morning," he continued, "that many of us were severely whipped for having been baptized the night before!" After we left them we heard the screams of these poor creatures while they were suffering under the blows of the hard treatment received from the overseers, for the crime, as we supposed, of talking with us. We felt thankful that we were exempted from such treatment, but we had no certainty that we should not, ere long be placed in a similar position.

On returning to the mill we met a young man, a relation of the owner of this plantation, who for some time had been eyeing us very attentively. He at length asked us if we had ever been whipped? and when I told him we had not, he replied, "well neither of you will ever be of any value." He expressed a good deal of surprise that we were allowed to wear hats and shoes, supposing that slaves had no business to wear such clothing as their master wore. We had carried our fishing lines with us and requested the privilege of fishing in his stream, which he roughly denied us, saying "we do not allow niggers to fish." Nothing daunted, however, by the rebuff, my brother went to another place, where, without asking permission of any one, he succeeded in obtaining a plentiful supply of fish and on returning, the young slave-holder seemed to be displeased at our success, but, knowing that we caught them in a stream which was not under his control, he said nothing. He knew that our master was a rich slave-holder and, probably, he guessed from our appearance that we were favourites of his, so perhaps he was somewhat induced, from that consideration, to let us alone, at any rate he did not molest us any more.

We afterwards carried our corn to a mill belonging to a Mr. Bullock, only about ten miles distant from our plantation. This man was very kind to us; if we were late at night he would take us into his house, give us beds to sleep upon, and take charge of our horses. He would even carry our grain himself into the mill; and he always furnished us in the morning with a good breakfast. We were rather astonished, for some time, that this man was so kind to us—and, in this respect, so different from the other miller—until we learned that he was not a slave-holder. This miller allowed us to catch as many fishes as we chose, and even furnished us with fishing implements when we had none, or only very imperfect ones, of our own.

While at this mill we became acquainted with a coloured man from a northern part of the country; and as our desire was strong to learn how our brethren fared in other places, we questioned him respecting his treatment. He complained much of his hard fate; he said he had a wife and one child, and begged for some of our fish to carry to his wife, which we gladly gave him. He told us he had just sent a few hickory nuts to market for which he had received 36 cents, and that he had given the money to his wife, to furnish her with some little articles of comfort.

On our return from their place, one time, we met with a coloured man and woman, who were very cross to each other. We inquired as to the cause of their disagreement and the man told us that the woman had such a tongue, and that some of them had taken a sheep because they did not get enough to eat, and this woman, after eating of it, went and told their master, and they had all received a severe whipping. This man enjoined upon his slaves never to steal from him again, but to steal as much as they chose from any other person: and if they took care to do it in such a manner, as the owner could not catch them in the act, nor be able to swear to the property after they had fetched it, he would shield them from punishment provided they would give him a share of the meat. Not long after this the slaves availing themselves of their master's protection, stole a pig from a neighbouring plantation, and, according to their agreement, furnished their master with his share. The owner of the missing animal, however, having heard something to make him suspect what had become of his property, came rushing into the house of the man who had just eaten of the stolen food, and in a very excited manner demanded reparation from him for the beast which his slaves had stolen; and the villain, rising from the table where he had just been eating of the stolen property, said, my servants know no more about your stolen hog than I do, which indeed was perfectly true, and the loser of the swine went away without saying any more; but although the master of this slave with whom we were talking, had told him that it was no sin to steal from others, my brother took good care to let him know, before we separated, that it was as much a sin in the sight of God to steal from the one as the other. "Oh," said the master, "niggers has nothing to do with God," and indeed the whole feature of slavery is so utterly inconsistent with the principles of religion, reason, and humanity, that it is no wonder that the very mention of the word God grates upon the ear as if it typefied the degeneracy of this hellish system.

Turn! great Ruler of the skies!
Turn from their sins thy searching eyes;
Nor let the offences of their hand,
Within thy book recorded stand.
There's not a sparrow or a worm
O'erlooked in thy decrees,
Thou raisest Monarchs to a throne—
They sink with equal ease.

May Christ's example, all divine,
To us a model prove!
Like his, O God! our hearts incline,
Our enemies to love![16]

⊰ CHAPTER III ⊱

My Master's son Charles, at one time, became impressed with the evils of slavery, and put his notion into practical effect by emancipating about forty of his slaves, and paying their expences to a free state. Our old master, about this time, being unable to attend to all his affairs himself, employed an overseer whose disposition was so cruel as to make many of the slaves run away. I fancy the neighbours began to clamour about our master's mild treatment to his slaves, for which reason he was induced to employ an overseer. The change in our treatment was so great, and so much for the worse, that we could not help lamenting that the master had adopted such a change. There is no telling what might have been the result of this new method amongst slaves, so unused to the lash as we were, if in the midst of the experiment our old master had not been called upon to go the way of all the earth. As he was about to expire he sent for my mother and me to come to his bedside; we ran with beating hearts and highly elated feelings, not doubting in the least but that he was about to confer upon us the boon of freedom—for we had both expected that we should be set free when master died—but imagine our deep disappointment when the old man called me to his side and said, Henry you will make a good Plough-boy, or a good gardener, now you must be an honest boy and never tell an untruth.

I have given you to my son William, and you must obey him; thus the old gentleman deceived us by his former kind treatment and raised expectation in our youthful minds which were doomed to be overthrown. He went to stand before the great Jehovah to give an account of the deeds done in the body, and we, disappointed in our expectations, were left to mourn, not so much our master's death, as our galling bondage. If there is any thing which tends to buoy up the spirit of the slave, under the pressure of his severe toils, more than another, it is the hope of future freedom: by this his heart is cheered and his soul is lighted up in the midst of the fearful scenes of agony and suffering which he has to endure. Occasionally, as some event approaches from which he can calculate on a relaxation of his sufferings, his hope burns with a bright blaze; but most generally the mind of the slave is filled with gloomy apprehension of a still harder fate. I have known many slaves to labour unusually hard with the view of obtaining the price of their own redemption, and, after they had paid for themselves over and over again, were—by the unprincipled tyranny and fiendish mockery of moral principle in which their barbarous masters delight to indulge—still refused what they had so fully paid for, and what they so ardently desired. Indeed a great many masters hold out to their slaves the object of purchasing their own freedom—in order to induce them to labour more—without at the same time, entertaining the slightest idea of ever fulfilling their promise.

On the death of my old master, his property was inherited by four sons, whose names were, Stronn, Charles, John, and William Barret;[17] so the human as well as every other kind of property, came to be divided equally amongst these four sons, which division—as it separated me from my father and mother, my sister and brother, with whom I had hitherto been allowed to live—was the most severe trial to my feelings which I had ever endured. I was then only 15 years of age, but it is as present in my mind as if but yesterday's sun had shone upon the dreadful exhibition. My mother was separated from her youngest child, and it was not till after she had begged most pitiously for its restoration, that she was allowed to give it one farewell embrace, before she had to let it go for ever. This kind of torture is a thousand fold more cruel and barbarous than the use of the lash which lacerates the back; the gashes which the whip, or the cow skin makes may heal, and the place which was marked, in a little while, may cease to exhibit the signs of what it had endured, but the pangs which lacerate the soul in consequence of the forcible disruption of parent and the dearest family ties, only grow deeper and more piercing, as memory fetches from a greater distance the horrid acts by which they have been produced. And there is no doubt but they under the weighty infirmities of declining life, and the increasing force and vividness with which the mind retains the memoranda of the agonies of former years—which form so great a part of memory's possessions in the minds of most slaves—hurry thousands annually from off the stage of life.

Mother, my sister Jane, and myself, fell into the hands of William Barret. My sister Mary and her children went another way; Edward, another, and John and Lewis and my sister Robinnet another. William Barret took my sister Martha for his "keep Miss." It is a difficult thing to divide all the slaves on a plantation; for no person wishes for all children, or all old people; while both old, young, and middle aged have to be divided:—but the tyrant slave-holder regards not the social, or domestic feelings of the slave, and makes his division according to the *moneyed* value they possess, without giving the slightest consideration to the domestic or social ties by which the individuals are bound to each other; indeed their common expression is, that "niggers have no feelings."

My father and mother were left on the plantation; but I was taken to the city of Richmond, to work in a tobacco manufactory, owned by my old master's son William, who had received a special charge from his father to take good care of me, and which charge my new master endeavoured to perform. He told me if I would behave well he would take good care of me and give me money to spend; he talked so kindly to me that I determined I would exert myself to the utmost to please him, and do just as he wished me in every respect. He furnished me with a new suit of clothes, and gave me money to buy things to send to my mother. One day I overheard him telling the overseer that *his father had raised me* — that I was a smart boy and that he must never whip me. I tried exceedingly hard to perform what I thought was my duty, and escaped the lash almost entirely, although I often thought the overseer would have liked to have given me a whipping, but my master's orders, which he dared not altogether to set aside, were my defence; so under these circumstances my lot was comparatively easy.

Our Overseer at that time was a coloured man, whose name was Wilson Gregory; he was generally considered a shrewd and sensible man, especially to be a man of colour; and, after the orders which my master gave him concerning me, he used to treat me very kindly indeed, and gave me board and lodgings in his own house. Gregory acted as book-keeper also to my master, and was much in favour with the merchants of the city and all who knew him; he instructed me how to judge of the qualities of tobacco, and with the view of making me a more proficient judge of that article, he advised me to learn to chew and to smoke which I therefore did.

About eighteen months after I came to the city of Richmond, an extraordinary occurrence took place which caused great excitement all over the town. I did not then know precisely what was the cause of this excitement, for I could get no satisfactory information from my master, only he said that some of the slaves had plotted to kill their owners. I have since learned that it was the famous Nat Turner's insurrection.[18] Many slaves were whipped, hung, and cut down with the swords in the streets; and some that were found away from their quarters after dark, were shot; the whole city was in the utmost excitement, and the whites seemed terrified beyond measure, so true it is that the "wicked flee when no man pursueth."[19] Great numbers of slaves were loaded with irons; some were half hung as it was termed—that is they were suspended from some tree with a rope about their necks, so adjusted as not quite to strangle them—and then they were pelted by men and boys with rotten eggs. This half-hanging is a refined species of punishment peculiar to slaves! This insurrection took place some distance from the city, and was the occasion of the enacting of that law by which more than five slaves were forbidden to meet together unless they were at work; and also of that, for the silencing all coloured preachers. One of that class in our city, refused to obey the impious mandate, and in consequence of his refusal, was severely whipped. His religion was, however, found to be too deeply rooted for him to be silenced by any mere power of man, and consequently, no efforts could avail to extort from his lips, a promise that he would cease to proclaim the glad tidings of the gospel to his enslaved and perishing fellow-men.

I had now been about two years in Richmond city, and not having, during that time, seen, and very seldom heard from, my mother, my feelings were very much tried by the separation which I had thus to endure. I missed severely her welcome smile when I returned from my daily task; no one seemed at that time to sympathise with me, and I began to feel, indeed, that I really was alone in the world; and worse than all, I could console myself with no hope, not even the most distant, that I should ever see my beloved parents again.

About this time Wilson Gregory, who was our overseer, died, and his place was supplied by a man named Stephen Bennett, who had a wooden leg; and who used to creep up behind the slaves to hear what they had to talk about in his absence; but his wooden leg generally betrayed him by coming into contact with something which would make a noise, and that would call the attention of the slaves to what he was about. He was a very mean man in all his ways, and was very much disliked by the slaves. He used to whip them, often, in a shameful manner. On one occasion I saw him take a slave, whose name was Pinkney, and make him take him off his shirt; he then tied his hands and gave him one hundred lashes on his bare back; and all this, because he lacked three pounds of his task, which was valued at six cents. I saw him do many other things which were equally cruel, but it would be useless to multiply instances here, as no rational being doubts that slavery, even in its mildest forms is a hard and cruel fate. Yet with all his barbarities and cruelties this man was generally reckoned a very sensible man in religious subjects, and he used to be frequently talking about things of that sort, but sometimes he spoke with very great levity indeed. He used to say that if he died and went to hell, he had enough of sense to fool the devil and get out. He did take his departure at last, to that bower, whence borne, no traveller returns, and whether well or ill prepared for the change, I will not say.

Bennett was followed as overseer, by one Henry Bedman, and he was the best that we had. He neither used the whip nor cheated the hands of what little they had to receive, and I am confident that he had more work done by equal numbers of hands, than had been done under any overseer either before or since his appointment to office. He possessed a much greater influence by his kindness than any overseer did by his lash. He was altogether a very good man; was very fond of sacred music, and used to ask me and some of the other slaves, who were working in the same room to sing for him — something "smart" as he used to say, which we were generally as well pleased to do, as he was to ask us: it was not our fate however to enjoy his kindness long, he too very soon died, and his death was looked upon as a misfortune by all who had been slaves under him.

⇥ CHAPTER IV ⇤

After the death of our lamented overseer we were placed under the care of one of the meanest and cruelest men that I ever knew; but before alluding particularly to his conduct, it may be interesting to describe the circumstances and condition of the slaves he had to superintend. The building in which I worked was about three hundred feet in length, and three stories high; affording room for two hundred people to work, but only one hundred and fifty were kept. One hundred and twenty of the persons employed were slaves, and the remainder free coloured people. We were obliged to work fourteen hours a day in the summer, and sixteen in the winter. One week consisted in separating the stems from the leaves of Tobacco; the leaves were then moistened with a fluid made from Liquorice and Sugar, which renders it not perfectly abhorrent to the taste of those who work it. These operations were performed by the women and boys, and after being thus moistened the leaves were then taken by the men and with the hands pressed into lumps and then twisted; it was then sent to what is called the machine house, and pressed into boxes and casks, whence it went to the sweat house and after lying about thirty days there, are taken out and shipped for the market.

The name of our overseer was John F. Allen; he was a thorough-going villain in all his modes of doing business; he was a savage looking sort of man; always apparently ready for any work of barbarity or cruelty to which the most depraved despot might call him. He understood how to turn a penny for his own advantage as well as any man. No person could match him in making a bargain; but whether he had acquired his low cunning from associating with that clan, or had it originally as one of the inherent properties of his diabolical disposition, I could not discover, but he excelled all I had ever seen in low mean trickery and artifice. He used to boast that by his shrewdness in managing the slaves, he made enough to support himself and family—and he had a very large family which I am sure consumed not less than one hundred dollars per annum—without touching one farthing of his own salary, which was fifteen hundred dollars per annum.

Mr. Allen used to rise very early in the morning, not that he might enjoy sweet communion with his own thoughts, or with his God; nor that he might further the *legitimate* interest of his master, but in order to look after matters which principally concerned himself; that was to rob his master and the poor slaves that were under his control, by every means in his power. His early rising was looked upon by our master as a token of great devotedness to his business; and as he was withall very pious and a member of the Episcopalian Church, my master seemed to place great confidence in him.[20] It was therefore no use for any of the workmen to complain to the master of anything the overseer did, for he would not listen to a word they said, but gave his sanction to his barbarous conduct in the fullest extent, no matter how tyrannical or unjust that conduct, or how cruel the punishments which he inflicted; so that that demon of an overseer was in reality our master.

As a specimen of Allen's cruelty I will mention the revolting case of a coloured man, who was frequently in the habit of singing. This man was taken sick, and although he had not made his appearance at the factory for two or three days, no notice was taken of him; no medicine was provided nor was there any physician employed to heal him. At the end of that time Allen ordered three men to go to the house of the invalid and fetch him to the factory; and of course, in a little while the sick man appeared; so feeble was he however from disease, that he was scarcely able to stand. Allen, notwithstanding, desired him to be stripped and his hands tied behind him; he was then tied to a large post and questioned about his singing; Allen told him that his singing consumed too much time, and that it hurt him very much, but that he was going to give him some medicine that would cure him; the poor trembling man made no reply and immediately the pious overseer Allen, for no other crime than sickness, inflicted two-hundred lashes upon his bare back; and even this might probably have been but a small part of his punishment, had not the poor man fainted away: and it was only then the blood-thirsty fiend ceased to apply the lash! I witnessed this transaction myself, but I durst not venture to say that the tyrant was doing wrong, because I was a slave and any interference on my part, would have led to a similar punishment upon myself. This poor man was sick for four weeks afterwards, during which time the weekly allowance, of seventy cents, for the hands to board themselves with, was withheld, and the poor man's wife had to support him in the best way she could, which in a land of slavery is no easy matter.

The advocates of slavery will sometimes tell us, that the slave is in better circumstances than he would be in a state of freedom, because he has a master to provide for him when he is sick; but even if this doctrine were true it would afford no argument whatever in favor of slavery; for no amount of kindness can be made the lawful price of any man's liberty, to infringe which is contrary to the laws of humanity and the decrees of God. But what is the real fact? In many instances the severe toils and exposures the slave has to endure at the will of his master, brings on his disease, and even then he is liable to the *lash for medicine*, and to live, or die by starvation as he may, without any support from his owner; for there is no law by which the master may be punished for his cruelty—by which he may be compelled to support his suffering slave.

My master knew all the circumstances of the case which I have just related, but he never interfered, nor even reproved the cruel overseer for what he had done; his motto was, Mr. Allen is always right, and so, right or wrong, whatever he did was law, and from his will there was no appeal.

I have before stated, that Mr. Allen was a very pious man—he was also a church member, but was much addicted to the habit of profane swearing—a vice which is, in slave countries, not at all uncommon in church members. He used particularly to expend his swearing breath in denunciation of the whole race of negroes—using more bad terms than I could here employ, without polluting the pen with which I write. Amongst the best epithets, were; "hogs," "dogs," "pigs," &c., &c.

At one time he was busily engaged in reading the Bible, when a slave came in who had been about ten minutes behind his time—precious time! Allen depended upon the punctuality of his slaves, for the support of his family, in the manner previously noticed: his anxiety to provide for his household, led him to indulge in a boisterous outbreak of anger; so that when the slave came in, he said, what are you so late for you black scamp? The poor man endeavoured to apologize for his lateness, but it was to no purpose. This professing christian proceeded to try the effects of the Bible on the slave's body, and actually dealt him a heavy blow in the face with the sacred book! But that not answering his purpose, and the man standing silent, he caught up a stick, and beat him with that. The slave afterwards complained to the master of the overseer's conduct, but was told that Mr. Allen would not do anything wrong.

Amongst Mr. Allen's other religious offices, he held that of superintendent of the Sunday school, where he used to give frequent exhortations to the slaves' children, in reference to their duty to their master. He told them they must never disobey their master, nor lie, nor steal, for if they did any of these, they would be sure to go to hell. But notwithstanding the deceitfulness of his character, and the fiendishness of his disposition, he was not, himself, perfectly proof against the influence of fear. One day it came on a heavy thunder storm; the clouds lowered heavily, and darkness usurped the dominion of day—it was so dark that the hands could not see to work, and I then began to converse with Mr. Allen about the storm. I asked him if it was not dangerous for the hands to work while the lightning flashed so terribly? He replied, he thought so, but he was placed there to keep them at their work, and he could not do otherwise. Just as we were speaking, a flash of lightning appeared to pass so close to us, that Mr. Allen jumped up from where he was sitting, and ran and locked himself up in a small room, where he supposed the lightning would not harm him. Some of the slaves said, they heard him praying that God would spare his life. That was a very severe storm, and a little while afterwards, we heard that a woman had been killed by the lightning. Although in the thunderstorm alluded to Mr. Allen seemed to be alarmed; at other times he did not appear to think seriously about such things, for I have heard him say, that he did not think God had anything to do with thunder and lightning. This same official had much apparent zeal in the cause of the Sunday school; he used to pray with, and for the children, and was indefatigable in teaching them the catechism after him; he was very particular, however, in not allowing them to hold the book in their own hands. His zeal did not appear to have any higher object than that of making the children more willing slaves; for he used frequently to tell his visitors that coloured people were never converted—that they had no souls, and could not go to heaven, but it was his duty to talk to them as he did! His liberality to the white people, was co-extensive with his denunciation of the coloured race; he said a white man may do what he pleased, and he could not be lost; he might lie, and rob the slaves, and do anything else, provided he read the Bible and joined the church!

⊰ CHAPTER V ⊱

It may now be proper to say a little about the state of the churches in slave countries. There was a Baptist minister in the city of Richmond, whose name was John Cave. I have heard this man declare in public that he had preached six years before he was converted and the reason of his conversion was as follows. He was in the habit of taking his glass of mint julep directly after prayers, or after preaching, which he thought wonderfully refreshed his soul and body; he would repeat the dram three or four times during the day. But an old slave of his, who had observed his practice hinted to him something about alternately drinking and preaching to the people; and, after thinking seriously on what the slave told him, he began to repent, and was converted. And now, he says he is truly converted, because his conscience reproved him for having made human beings articles of traffic; but I believe his second conversion is just about as complete as his first, for although he owed the second change to one of his own slaves, and ever confessed that the first effect of his conversion, was, to open up to his conscience the evil of the traffic in human beings, instead of letting those at liberty which he had under his control—and which might have been at once expected, as a natural consequence of his conviction—he endeavoured to apologize for the want of conscience, by finding, what he called, a good master for them, and selling them all to him.

But the religion of the slave-holder is everywhere a system of mere delusion, got up expressly for the purpose of deceiving the poor slaves, for everywhere the leading doctrine in the slave-holders' religion is, that it is the duty of the slave to obey his master in all things.

When Mr. Cave left the city he was succeeded by a Mr. Jeter, who remained for many years; but at the time when he commenced his ministerial duties, many of the slaves were running away to free states; on the learning of which Mr. Jeter's first object was to devise some plan by which the masters could more effectively prevent their negroes from escaping; and the result of his ingenuity was as follows. He got the deacons and many more of the good christians of his church, whether to believe or not I do not know, but to hold out that the place of meeting which they then occupyed was not large enough for them; and he seemed not to relish being in the same church with the negroes, but, however that was, he managed, with the assistance of his church members, to get the negroes all round the district to believe that out of love for them, and from pure regard to their spiritual interests, it had been agreed that the old meeting house was to be given to the negroes for their own use, on their paying a small portion of the price at which it was estimated. The church was valued at 13,000 dollars, but they would only be required to pay 3,000 dollars in order to have it for themselves. The negroes were pleased with the idea of having a place of meeting for themselves, and so were induced to save every cent they could to buy the chapel. They were thus provided with a strong motive for remaining where they were, and also by means of this pious fraud, which it afterwards proved itself to be, they were deprived of such little sums of money as might occasionally drop into their hands, and with which they might have been assisted in effecting their escape. These resolutions were punctually carried into effect; a splendid new church was built for the whites; and it was made a rule of that church, that if any coloured person entered it, without special business, he was liable to be taken to the watch-house and to receive 39 lashes! The negroes paid what was at first demanded of them for the old building, but when they wished to get it placed entirely in their hands, they were charged with a still further sum; and after they had paid that, they had still more to pay, and never, so long as I was there, got possession of the church, and probably never will. A minister was, however, appointed to preach for them beside the one that preached for the white people.

A man named Knopp who came from the north preached once

in the church of the negroes.[21] He took for his text, *"O! Jerusalem, Jerusalem which killest the prophets and stonest them that are sent unto thee, how often would I have gathered thee as a hen gathereth her chickens under her wings, and ye would not."*[22] Mr. Jeter and the members of the whites' church were so offended at this man's sermon, that they went in a body to his lodgings and were about to mob him, if he had not been defended by a number of his own friends; but I believe if he had been left to the tender mercies of this professed servant of the Most High, and his christian associates, he would never have escaped with his life.[23]

The Rev. R. Ryland, who preached for the coloured people, was professor at the Baptist seminary near the city of Richmond, and the coloured people had to pay him a salary of 700 dollars per annum, although they neither chose him nor had the least control over him.[24] He did not consider himself bound to preach regularly, but only when he was not otherwise engaged, so he preached about 40 sermons a year and was a zealous supporter of the slaveholders' cause; and, so far as I could judge, he had no notion whatever of the pure religion of Jesus Christ. He used to preach from such texts as that in the epistle to the Ephesians, where St. Paul says, "servants be obedient to them that are your masters and mistresses according to the flesh, and submit to them with fear and trembling";[25] he was not ashamed to invoke the authority of heaven in support of the slave-degrading laws under which masters could with impunity abuse their fellow-creatures.

⊰ CHAPTER VI ⊱

I now began to think of entering the matrimonial state; and with that view I had formed an acquaintance with a young woman named Nancy, who was a slave belonging to a Mr. Leigh a clerk in the Bank, and, like many more slave-holders, professing to be a very pious man. We had made it up to get married, but it was necessary in the first place, to obtain our masters' permission, as we could do nothing without their consent. I therefore went to Mr. Leigh, and made known to him my wishes, when he told me he never meant to sell Nancy, and if my master would agree never to sell me, I might marry her. He promised faithfully that he would not sell her, and pretended to entertain an extreme horror of separating families. He gave me a note to my master, and after they had discussed the matter over, I was allowed to marry the object of my choice. When she became my wife she was living with a Mr. Reevs, a minister of the gospel, who had not long come from the north, where he had the character of being an Antislavery man; but he had not been long in the south when all his anti-slavery notions vanished and he became a staunch advocate of slave-holding doctrines, and even wrote articles in favour of slavery which were published in the *Richmond Republican*.

My wife was still the property of Mr. Leigh and, from the apparent sincerity of his promises to us, we felt confident that he would not separate us. We had not, however, been married above twelve months, when his conscientious scruples vanished, and he sold my wife to a Mr. Joseph H. Colquitt, a saddler, living in the city of Richmond, and a member of Dr. Plummer's church there. This Mr. Colquitt was an exceedingly cruel man, and he had a wife who was, if possible, still more cruel. She was very contrary and hard to be pleased; she used to abuse my wife very much, not because she did not do her duty, but because, it was said, her manners were too refined for a slave. At this time my wife had a child and this vexed Mrs. Colquitt very much; she could not bear to see her nursing her baby and used to wish some great calamity to happen to my wife. Eventually she was so much displeased with my wife that she induced Mr. Colquitt to sell her to one Philip M. Tabb, Junr. for the sum of 450 dollars; but coming to see the value of her more clearly after she tried to do without her, she could not rest till she got Mr. Colquitt to repurchase her from Mr. Tabb, which he did in about four months after he had sold her, for 500 dollars, being 50 more than he had sold her for.

Shortly after this Mr. Colquitt was taken sick, and his minister, the Rev. Dr. Plummer, was sent for to visit him; the doctor came and prayed for him and so did other members of the church; but he did not get any better so that they all thought he must soon die; the doctors had given up all hopes of him, and his wife and children, and friends, stood round his bedside in tears, expecting every minute he would breathe his last. All the servants were in readiness lest they should be called to go on some message. I had just then got home from labouring for my master; my wife was waiting for me, but she said she expected, every minute, that some person would be calling to tell her that master was gone, when, to my surprise, Joseph Colquitt sent to my wife to tell me to come and speak with him. I immediately left my room and went to his bed-side; and as soon as he saw me he caught hold of my hand and said;—"Henry will you pray for me and ask the Lord to spare my life, and restore me to health?" I felt it my duty to do the best I could in asking the Lord to have mercy upon him, because, although he was a slave-holder, and a very cruel man, and had used my wife very badly, yet I had no right to judge between him and his God, so I knelt down by his bed-side and prayed for him. After I got up he caught hold of my arm again and said, "one more favour I have to ask of you—go and tell all my slaves that belong to the church to come and pray for me." I went, according to his request, and we prayed three nights with him, after our work was done, and although we needed rest ourselves, yet at the earnest desire of the apparently dying man we were induced to forego our rest, and to spend our time in comforting him. At the end of this time he began to get a little better, and in a few weeks he was able to sit at table, and to take his meals with the family. I happened to be at his house one day, at our breakfast hour, after he got quite well, and his wife appeared as if she wished to joke her husband about the coloured people praying for him when he was sick. Mrs. Colquitt had been expelled from the Baptist church, and since that time she had disliked religion. She pretended that she did not believe either in God or Devil, and went on at such a rate, plaguing Mr. Colquitt, about the negroes praying for him, that he grew angry at last and exclaimed with an oath that it was all lies about the negroes praying for him; he denied asking any person to pray for him, and he said if he did ask the negroes to pray for him he must have been out of his senses, and did not, at the time he spoke, remember anything about it; but his wife still persisting in what she said, he went to the back door and calling his slaves one at a time, asked them who it was that prayed for him, until he got the names of all those who had been concerned in the affair, and when he had done so, he whipped every one of them which said he had prayed as Mrs. Colquitt had stated. He seemed wishful to whip me also, but, as I did not belong to him, he was deprived of the pleasure of paying me for my services in the manner, in which others had been rewarded. Mr. Colquitt, however, determined that I should suffer too, and for that purpose he proceeded to sell my wife to one Samuel Cottrell, who wished to purchase her. Cottrell was a saddler and had a shop in Richmond. This man came to me one day and told me that Mr. Colquitt was going to sell my wife, and stated that he wanted a woman to wait upon his wife, and he thought my wife would precisely suit her; but he said her master asked 650 dollars for her and her children, and he had only 600 that he could conveniently spare but if I would let him have fifty, to make up the price, he would prevent her from being sold away from me. I was, however, a little suspicious about being fooled out of my money, and I asked him if I did advance the money what security I could have that he would not sell my wife as the others had done; but he said to me "do you think if you allow me to have that money, that I could have the heart to sell your wife to any other person but yourself, and particularly knowing that your wife is my sister and you my brother in the Lord; while all of us are members of the church? *Oh! no*, I never could have the heart to do such a deed as that." After he had shown off his religion in this manner, and lavished it upon me, I thought I would let him have the money, not that I had implicit faith in his promise, but that I knew he could purchase her if he wished whether I were to assist him or not, and I thought by thus bringing him under an obligation to me it might at least be somewhat to the advantage of my wife and to me; so I gave him the 50 dollars and he went off and bought my wife and children: — and that very same day he came to me and told me, that my wife and children were now his property, and that I must hire a house for them and he would allow them to live there if I would furnish them with everything they wanted, and pay him 50 dollars a year; "if you don't do this," he said, "I will sell her as soon as I can get a buyer for her." I was struck with astonishment to think that this man, in one day, could exhibit himself in two such different characters. A few hours ago filled with expressions of love and kindness, and now a monster tyrant, making light of the most social ties and imposing such terms as he chose on those whom, but a little before, had begged to conform to his will. Now, being a slave, I had no power to hire a house, and what this might have resulted in I do not know, if I had not met with a friend in the time of need, in the person of James C. A. Smith, Jr.[26] He was a free man and I went to him and told him my tale and asked him to go and hire a house for me, to put my wife and children into; which he immediately did. He hired one at 72 dollars per annum, and stood master of it for me; and, notwithstanding the fearful liabilities under which I lay, I now began to feel a little easier, and might, perhaps, have managed to live in a kind of a way if we had been let alone here. But Mr. S. Cottrell had not yet done with robbing us; he no sooner saw that we were thus comfortably situated, than he said my wife must do some of his washing. I still had to pay the house hire, and the hire of my wife; to find her and the children with everything they required, and she had to do his washing beside. Still we felt ourselves more comfortable than we had ever been before. In this way, we went on for some time: I paid him the hire of my wife regularly, whenever he called for it—whether it was due or not—but he seemed still bent on robbing me more thoroughly than he had the previous day; for one pleasant morning, in the month of August, 1848, when my wife and children, and myself, were sitting at table, about to eat our breakfast, Mr. Cottrell called, and said, he wanted some money to day, as he had a demand for a large amount. I said to him, you know I have no money to spare, because it takes nearly all that I make for myself, to pay my wife's hire, the rent of my house, my own ties to my master, and to keep ourselves in meat and clothes; and if at any time, I have made anything more than that, I have paid it to you in advance, and what more can I do? Mr. Cottrell, however, said, "I want money, and money I will have." I could make him no answer; he then went away. I then said to my wife, "I wonder what Mr. Cottrell means by saying I want money and money I will have," my poor wife burst into tears and said perhaps he will sell one of our little children, and our hearts were so full that neither of us could eat any breakfast, and after mutually embracing each other, as it might be our last meeting, and fondly pressing our little darlings to our bosoms, I left the house and went off to my daily labour followed by my little children who called after me to come back soon. I felt that life had joys worth living for if I could only be allowed to enjoy them, but my heart was filled with deep anguish from the awful calamity, which I was thus obliged to contemplate, as not only a possible but a highly probable occurrence. I now went away to my work and I could as I went see many other slaves hastening in the same direction. I began to consider their lot and mine, and although my heart was filled with sorrow I felt still disposed to look upon the bright side of the future. I could still see some alleviation to my case of sorrow; it was true that the greater portion of my earnings were stolen from me by the unscrupulous hand of my master; that I was entirely at his mercy, and might at any moment be snatched from those enjoyments as well as those I thought were open to me; that if he chose he might still further gratify his robbing propensities and demand a larger portion of my earnings; so that the pleasures of intellect would be completely closed to my mind, but I could enjoy myself with my family about me while I listened to the pleasing prattle of my children, and experience the kindness of a wife, which were privileges that every slave could not enjoy.

I had not been many hours at my work, when I was informed that my wife and children were taken from their home, sent to the auction mart and sold, and then lay in prison ready to start away the next day for North Carolina with the man who had purchased them. I cannot express, in language, what were my feelings on this occasion. My master treated me kindly but he still retained me in a state of slavery. His kindness, however, did not keep me from feeling the smart of this awful deprivation. I had left my wife and children at home in the morning as well situated as slaves could be; I was not anticipating their loss, not on account of the feigned piety of their owner, for I had long ago learned to look through such hollow pretences in those who held slaves, but because of the obligation to me for money I had advanced to him, *on the expressed condition that he should not sell her to any person but myself*; such, however, was the case, and as soon as I could get away, I went and purchased some things to take to the jail to them I so much loved; and to have one farewell embrace before parting for ever. I had not proceeded far, however, when I met with a gentleman who perceiving my anguish of heart, as depicted in my countenance, inquired what was the matter with me. I had no sooner hinted at my circumstances, however, than he knew all about it, having heard it, before. He advised me not to go the jail, "for," said he, "the man that bought your wife and family has told your master some falsehoods and has ordered the jailor to seize you and put you in prison if you should make your appearance there; when you would most likely be sold separately from them, because the *Methodist Minister* that bought your wife, does not want any men," so being thus advised I thought it better not to go to the jail myself, but I procured a friend to go in my stead, and take some money and the things which I had purchased for my wife, and tell her how it was that I could not come myself. And it turned out in the end to be much better that I did not go, for as soon as the young man arrived at the jail he was seized and put in prison, the jailor mistaking him for me: but when he discovered his mistake he was very angry and vented his rage upon the innocent youth by kicking him out of the prison. He discovered his mistake by asking my wife if that were not her husband, she said he was not; but he was not satisfied with her answer for he asked the children also if he were not their father, and as they too said no he was convinced, and then proceeded to abuse the young man in the manner before mentioned.

After I had heard of these things, I went to my *christian* master and informed him how I was served, but he shoved me away from him as if I was not human. I could not rest with this, however, I went to him a second time and implored him to be kind enough to buy my wife and to save me from so much trouble of mind; still he was inexorable and only answered me by telling me to go to my work and not bother him any more. I went to him a *third* time, which would be about ten o'clock and told him how Cottrell had robbed me, as this scoundrel was not satisfied with selling my wife and children, but he had no sooner got them out of the town than he took everything which he could find in my house and carried it off to be sold; the things which he then took had cost me nearly three hundred dollars. I begged master to write Cottrell and make him give me up my things, but his answer was Mr. Cottrell is a gentleman; I am afraid to meddle with his business. So having satisfied myself that the master would do nothing for me, I left him and went to two young gentlemen with whom I was acquainted to try if I could induce them to buy my wife; but when I had stated my case to them they gave me to understand that they did not deal in slaves so they could not do that, but they expressed their willingness to do anything else that I might desire of them; so finding myself unsuccessful here, I went sorrowfully back to my own deserted home, and found that what I had heard was quite true; not only had my wife and children been taken away, but every article of furniture had also been removed to the auction mart to be sold. I then made inquiry as to where my things had been put; and having found this out went to the sheriff's office and informed him, that the things Mr. Cottrell had brought to be sold did not belong to him, but that they were mine, and I hoped he would return them to me. I was then told by the sheriff that Mr. Cottrell had left the things to be sold in order to pay himself a debt of seventeen dollars and twenty-one cents, which he said if I would pay he would let me take away the things. I then went to my good friend Doctor Smith who was always ready and willing to do what he could for me, and having got the money, I paid it to the sheriff and took away the things which I was obliged to do that night, as far as I was able, and what were left I removed in the morning. When I was taking home the last of my things I met Mr. Cottrell, and two of his Christian brethren, in the street. He stopped me and said he had heard I had been to the sheriff's office and got away my things. Yes I said I have been and got away *my things* but I could not get away *my wife and children* whom you have put beyond my power to redeem. He then began to give me a round of abuse, while his two Christian friends stood by and heard him, but they did not seem to be the least offended at the terrible barbarity which was there placed before them.

I now left Mr. Cottrell and his friends, and going home, endeavoured to court a little rest by lying down in a position so as to induce sleep. I had borne too heavy a load of grief on my mind to admit of me even closing my eyes for an hour during the whole night. Many schemes for effecting the redemption of my family passed through my mind, but when the morning's sun arose I found myself on my way towards my master's house, to make another attempt to induce him to purchase my wife. But although I besought him, with tears in my eyes, I did not succeed in making the least impression on his obdurate heart, and he utterly refused to advance the smallest portion of the 5000 dollars I had paid him in order to relieve my sufferings, and yet he was a church member of considerable standing in Richmond. He even told me that I could get another wife and so I need not trouble myself about that one; but I told him those that God had joined together let no man put assunder,[27] and that I did not want another wife, but my own whom I had loved so long. The mentioning of the passage of scripture seemed to give him much offence for he instantly drove me from his house saying he did not wish to hear that!

My agony was now complete, she with whom I had travelled the journey of life *in chains*, for the space of twelve years, and the dear little pledges God had given us I could see plainly must now be separated from me for ever, and I must continue, desolate and alone, to drag my chains through the world. O dear, I thought, shall my wife and children no more greet my sight with their cheerful looks and happy smiles! for far away in the North Carolina swamps are they henceforth to toil beneath the scorching rays of a hot sun deprived of a husband's and a father's care! Can I endure such agony—shall I stay behind while they are thus driven with the tyrant's rod? I must stay, I am a slave, the law of men gives me no power to ameliorate my condition; it shuts up every avenue of hope; but, thanks be to God, there is a law of heaven which senates' laws cannot control!

While I was thus musing I received a message, that if I wished to see my wife and children, and bid them the last farewell, I could do so, by taking my stand on the street where they were all to pass on their way for North Carolina. I quickly availed myself of this information, and placed myself by the side of a street, and soon had the melancholy satisfaction of witnessing the approach of a gang of slaves, amounting to three hundred and fifty in number, marching under the direction of a methodist minister, by whom they were purchased, and amongst which slaves were my wife and children. I stood in the midst of many who, like myself, were mourning the loss of friends and relations and had come there to obtain one parting look at those whose company they but a short time before had imagined they should always enjoy, but who were, without any regard to their own wills, now driven by the tyrant's voice and the smart of the whip on their way to another scene of toil, and, to them, another land of sorrow in a far off southern country. These beings were marched with ropes about their necks, and staples on their arms, and, although in that respect the scene was no very novel one to me, yet the peculiarity of my own circumstances made it assume the appearance of unusual horror. This train of beings was accompanied by a number of wagons loaded with little children of many different families, which as they appeared rent the air with their shrieks and cries and vain endeavours to resist the separation which was thus forced upon them, and the cords with which they were thus bound; but what should I now see in the very foremost wagon but a little child looking towards me and pitifully calling, father! father! This was my eldest child, and I was obliged to look upon it for the last time that I should, perhaps, ever see it again in life; if it had been going to the grave and this gloomy procession had been about to return its body to the dust from whence it sprang, whence its soul had taken its departure for the land of spirits, my grief would have been nothing in comparison to what I then felt; for then I could have reflected that its sufferings were over and that it would never again require nor look for a father's care; but now it goes with all those tender feelings riven, by which it was endeared to a father's love; it must still live subjected to the deprivation of paternal care and to the chains and wrongs of slavery, and yet be dead to the pleasure of a father from whose heart the impression of its early innocence and love will never be effaced. Thus passed my child from my presence—it was my own child—I loved it with all the fondness of a father; but things were so ordered that I could only say, farewell, and leave it to pass in its chains while I looked for the approach of another gang in which my wife was also loaded with chains. My eye soon caught her precious face, but, gracious heavens! that glance of agony may God spare me from ever again enduring! My wife, under the influence of her feelings, jumped aside; I seized hold of her hand while my mind felt unutterable things, and my tongue was only able to say, we shall meet in heaven! I went with her for about four miles hand in hand, but both our hearts were so overpowered with feeling that we could say nothing, and when at last we were obliged to part, the look of mutual love which we exchanged was all the token which we could give each other that we should yet meet in heaven.

⊰ CHAPTER VII ⊱

I had for a long while been a member of the choir in the Affeviar church in Richmond, but after the severe family affliction to which I have just alluded in the last chapter and the knowledge that these cruelties were perpetrated by ministers and church members, I began strongly to suspect the christianity of the slave-holding church members and hesitated much about maintaining my connection with them. The suspicion of these slave-dealing christians was the means of keeping me absent from all their churches from the time that my wife and children were torn from me, until Christmas day in the year 1848; and I would not have gone then but being a leading member of the choir, I yielded to the entreaties of my associates to assist at a concert of sacred music which was to be got up for the benefit of the church. My friend Dr. Smith, who was the conductor of the under-ground railway, was also a member of the choir, and when I had consented to attend he assisted me in selecting twenty-four pieces to be sung on the occasion.

On the day appointed for our concert I went along with

Dr. Smith, and the singing commenced at half-past three o'clock, p.m. When we had sung about ten pieces and were engaged in singing the following verse—

> Again the day returns of holy rest,
> Which, when he made the world, Jehovah blest;
> When, like his own, he bade our labours cease,
> And all be piety, and all be peace,[28]

the members were rather astonished at Dr. Smith, who stood on my right hand, suddenly closing his book, and sinking down upon his seat, his eyes being at the same time filled with tears. Several of them began to inquire what was the matter with him, but he did not tell them. I guessed what it was and afterwards found out that I had judged of the circumstances correctly. Dr. Smith's feelings were overcome with a sense of doing wrongly in singing for the purpose of obtaining money to assist those who were buying and selling their fellow-men. He thought at that moment he felt reproved by Almighty God for lending his aid to the cause of slave-holding religion; and it was under this impression he closed his book and formed the resolution which he still acts upon, of never singing again or taking part in the services of a pro-slavery church. He is now in New England publicly advocating the cause of emancipation.

After we had sung several other pieces we commenced the anthem, which run thus—

> Vital spark of heavenly flame,
> Quit, O! quit the mortal frame,—[29]

These words awakened in me feelings in which the sting of former sufferings was still sticking fast, and stimulated by the example of Dr. Smith, whose feelings I read so correctly, I too made up my mind that I would be no longer guilty of assisting those bloody dealers in the bodies and souls of men; and ever since that time I have steadfastly kept my resolution.

I now began to get weary of my bonds; and earnestly panted

after liberty. I felt convinced that I should be acting in accordance with the will of God, if I could snap in sunder those bonds by which I was held body and soul as the property of a fellow man. I looked forward to the good time which every day I more and more firmly believed would yet come, when I should walk the face of the earth in full possession of all that freedom which the finger of God had so clearly written on the constitutions of man, and which was common to the human race; but of which, by the cruel hand of tyranny, I, and millions of my fellow-men, had been robbed.

I was well acquainted with a storekeeper in the city of Richmond, from whom I used to purchase my provisions; and having formed a favourable opinion of his integrity, one day in the course of a little conversation with him, I said to him if I were free I would be able to do business such as he was doing; he then told me that my occupation (a tobacconist) was a money-making one, and if I were free I had no need to change for another.[30] I then told him my circumstances in regard to my master, having to pay him 25 dollars per month, and yet that he refused to assist me in saving my wife from being sold and taken away to the South, where I should never see her again; and even refused to allow me to go and see her until my hours of labour were over. I told him this took place about five months ago, and I had been meditating my escape from slavery since, and asked him, as no person was near us, if he could give me any information about how I should proceed. I told him I had a little money and if he would assist me I would pay him for so doing. The man asked me if I was not afraid to speak that way to him; I said no, for I imagined he believed that every man had a right to liberty. He said I was quite right, and asked me how much money I would give him if he would assist me to get away. I told him that I had 166 dollars and that I would give him the half; so we ultimately agreed that I should have his service in the attempt for 86. Now I only wanted to fix upon a plan. He told me of several plans by which others had managed to effect their escape, but none of them exactly suited my taste. I then left him to think over what would be best to be done, and, in the mean time, went to consult my friend Dr. Smith, on the subject. I mentioned the plans which the storekeeper had suggested, and as he did not approve either of them very much, I still looked for some plan which would be more certain and more safe, but I was determined that come what may, I should have my freedom or die in the attempt.

One day, while I was at work, and my thoughts were eagerly feasting upon the idea of freedom, I felt my soul called out to heaven to breathe a prayer to Almighty God. I prayed fervently that he who seeth in secret and knew the inmost desires of my heart, would lend me his aid in bursting my fetters asunder, and in restoring me to the posession of those rights, of which men had robbed me; when the idea suddenly flashed across my mind of shutting myself *up in a box*, and getting myself conveyed as dry goods to a free state.

Being now satisfied that this was the plan for me, I went to my friend Dr. Smith and, having acquainted him with it, we agreed to have it put at once into execution, not however without calculating the chances of danger with which it was attended; but buoyed up by the prospect of freedom and increased hatred to slavery I was willing to dare even death itself rather than endure any longer the clanking of those galling chains. It being still necessary to have the assistance of the storekeeper, to see that the box was kept in its right position on its passage, I then went to let him know my intention, but he said although he was willing to serve me in any way he could, he did not think I could live in a box for so long a time as would be necessary to convey me to Philadelphia, but as I had already made up my mind, he consented to accompany me and keep the box right all the way.

My next object was to procure a box, and with the assistance of a carpenter that was very soon accomplished, and taken to the place where the packing was to be performed. In the mean time the storekeeper had written to a friend in Philadelphia, but as no answer had arrived, we resolved to carry out our purpose as best we could. It was deemed necessary that I should get permission to be absent from my work for a few days, in order to keep down suspicion until I had once fairly started on the road to liberty; and as I had then a gathered finger I thought that would form a very good excuse for obtaining leave of absence; but when I showed it to one overseer, Mr. Allen, he told me it was not so bad as to prevent me from working, so with a view of making it bad enough, I got Dr. Smith to procure for me some oil of vitriol[31] in order to drop a little of this on it, but in my hurry I dropped rather much and made it worse than there was any occasion for, in fact it was very soon eaten in to the bone, and on presenting it again to Mr. Allen I obtained the permission required, with the advice that I should go home and get a poultice of flax-meal to it, and keep it well poulticed until it got better. I took him instantly at his word and went off directly to the storekeeper who had by this time received an answer from his friend in Philadelphia, and had obtained permission to address the box to him, this friend in that city, arranging to call for it as soon as it should arrive. There being no time to be lost, the storekeeper, Dr. Smith, and myself, agreed to meet next morning at four o'clock, in order to get the box ready for the express train. The box which I had procured was three feet one inch wide, two feet six inches high, and two feet wide: and on the morning of the 29th day of March, 1849, I went into the box—having previously bored three gimlet holes opposite my face, for air, and provided myself with a bladder of water, both for the purpose of quenching my thirst and for wetting my face, should I feel getting faint. I took the gimlet also with me, in order that I might bore more holes if I found I had not sufficient air. Being thus equipped for the battle of liberty, my friends nailed down the lid and had me conveyed to the Express Office, which was about a mile distant from the place where I was packed. I had no sooner arrived at the office than I was turned heels up, while some person nailed something on the end of the box. I was then put upon a wagon and driven off to the depôt with my head down, and I had no sooner arrived at the depôt, than the man who drove the wagon tumbled me roughly into the baggage car, where, however, I happened to fall on my right side.

The next place we arrived at was Potomac Creek, where the baggage had to be removed from the cars, to be put on board the steamer; where I was again placed with my head down, and in this dreadful position had to remain nearly an hour and a half, which, from the sufferings I had thus to endure, seemed like an age to me, but I was forgetting the battle of liberty, and I was resolved to conquer or die. I felt my eyes swelling as if they would burst from their sockets; and the veins on my temples were dreadfully distended with pressure of blood upon my head. In this position I attempted to lift my hand to my face but I had no power to move it; I felt a cold sweat coming over me which seemed to be a warning that death was about to terminate my earthly miseries, but as I feared even that, less than slavery, I resolved to submit to the will of God, and, under the influence of that impression, I lifted up my soul in prayer to God, who alone, was able to deliver me. My cry was soon heard, for I could hear a man saying to another, that he had travelled a long way and had been standing there two hours, and he would like to get somewhat to sit down; so perceiving my box, standing on end, he threw it down and then two sat upon it. I was thus relieved from a state of agony which may be more easily imagined than described. I could now listen to the men talking, and heard one of them asking the other what he supposed *the box contained*; his companion replied he guessed it was "THE MAIL." I too thought it was a mail but not such a mail as he supposed it to be.

The next place at which we arrived was the city of Washington, where I was taken from the steam-boat, and again placed upon a wagon and carried to the depôt right side up with care; but when the driver arrived at the depôt I heard him call for some person to help to take the box off the wagon, and some one answered him to the effect that he might throw it off; but, says the driver, it is marked "this side up with care;" so if I throw it off I might break something; the other answered him that it did not matter if he broke all that was in it, the railway company were able enough to pay for it. No sooner were these words spoken than I began to tumble from the wagon, and falling on the end where my head was, I could hear my neck give a crack, as if it had been snapped asunder, and I was knocked completely insensible. The first thing I heard, after that, was some person saying, "there is no room for the box, it will have to remain and be sent through to-morrow with the luggage train"; but the Lord had not quite forsaken me, for in answer to my earnest prayer He so ordered affairs that I should not be left behind; and I now heard a man say that the box had come with the express, and it must be sent on. I was then tumbled into the car with my head downwards again, but the car had not proceeded far before, more luggage having to be taken in, my box got shifted about and so happened to turn upon its right side; and in this position I remained till I got to Philadelphia, of our arrival in which place I was informed by hearing some person say, "We are in port and at Philadelphia." My heart then leaped for joy, and I wondered if any person knew that such a box was there.

Here it may be proper to observe that the man who had promised to accompany my box failed to do what he promised; but, to prevent it remaining long at the station after its arrival, he sent a telegraphic message to his friend, and I was only twenty-seven hours in the box, though travelling a distance of three hundred and fifty miles.

I was now placed in the depôt amongst the other luggage, where I lay till seven o'clock, P.M., at which time a wagon drove up, and I heard a person inquire for such a box as that in which I was. I was then placed on a wagon and conveyed to the house where my friend in Richmond had arranged I should be received. A number of persons soon collected round the box after it was taken in to the house, but as I did not know what was going on I kept myself quiet. I heard a man say, "let us rap upon the box and see if he is alive"; and immediately a rap ensued and a voice said, tremblingly, "Is all right within?" to which I replied — "all right." The joy of the friends was very great; when they heard that I was alive they soon managed to break open the box, and then came my resurrection from the grave of slavery. I rose a freeman, but I was too weak, by reason of long confinement in that box, to be able to stand, so I immediately swooned away. After my recovery from the swoon the first thing, which arrested my attention, was the presence of a number of friends, every one seeming more anxious than another, to have an opportunity of rendering me their assistance, and of bidding me a hearty welcome to the possession of my natural rights. I had risen as it were from the dead; I felt much more than I could readily express; but as the kindness of Almighty God had been so conspicuously shown in my deliverance, I burst forth into the following hymn of thanksgiving,

> I waited patiently, I waited patiently for the Lord, for the
>   Lord;
> And he inclined unto me, and heard my calling:
> I waited patiently, I waited patiently for the Lord,
> And he inclined unto me, and heard my calling:
> And he hath put a new song in my mouth,
> Even a thanksgiving, even a thanksgiving, even a
>   thanksgiving unto our God.
> Blessed, Blessed, Blessed, Blessed is the man, Blessed is the
>   man,
> Blessed is the man that hath set his hope, his hope in the
>   Lord;
> O Lord my God, Great, Great, Great,
> Great are the wondrous works which thou hast done.
> Great are the wondrous works which thou hast done, which
>   thou hast done:
> If I should declare them and speak of them, they would be
>   more, more, more than I am able to express.
> I have not kept back thy loving kindness and truth from the
>   great congregation.
> I have not kept back thy loving kindness and truth from the
>   great congregation.
> Withdraw not thou thy mercy from me,
> Withdraw not thou thy mercy from me, O Lord;
> Let thy loving kindness and thy truth always preserve me,
> Let all those that seek thee be joyful and glad,
> Let all those that seek thee be joyful and glad, be joyful, and
>   glad, be joyful and glad, be joyful, be joyful, be joyful, be
>   joyful, be joyful and glad—be glad in thee.
> And let such as love thy salvation,
> And let such as love thy salvation, say, always,
> The Lord be praised,

The Lord be praised.
Let all those that seek thee be joyful and glad,
And let such as love thy salvation, say always,
The Lord be praised,
The Lord be praised,
The Lord be praised.[32]

I was then taken by the hand and welcomed to the houses of the following friends:—Mr. J. Miller, Mr. M'Kim, Mr. and Mrs. Motte,[33] Mr. and Mrs. Davis,[34] and many others, by all of whom I was treated in the kindest manner possible. But it was thought proper that I should not remain long in Philadelphia, so arrangements were made for me to proceed to Massachusetts, where, by the assistance of a few Anti-slavery friends, I was enabled shortly after to arrive. I went to New York, where I became acquainted with Mr. H. Long,[35] and Mr. Eli Smith, who were very kind to me the whole time I remained there. My next journey was to New Bedford, where I remained some weeks under the care of Mr. H. Ricketson,[36] my finger being still bad from the effects of the oil of vitriol with which I dressed it before I left Richmond. While I was here I heard of a great Anti-slavery meeting which was to take place in Boston, and being anxious to identify myself with that public movement, I proceeded there and had the pleasure of meeting the hearty sympathy of thousands to whom I related the story of my escape. I have since attended large meetings in different towns in the states of Maine, New Hampshire, Vermont, Connecticut, Rhode Island, Pennsylvania, and New York, in all of which places I have found many friends and have endeavoured, according to the best of my abilities, to advocate the cause of the emancipation of the slave; with what success I will not pretend to say—but with a daily increasing confidence in the humanity and justice of my cause, and in the assurance of the approbation of Almighty God.

I have composed the following song in commemoration of my fete in the box:—

Air:—"UNCLE NED."[37]

I.

Here you see a man by the name of Henry Brown,
Ran away from the South to the North;
Which he would not have done but they stole all his rights,
But they'll never do the like again.

Chorus—Brown laid down the shovel and the hoe,
   Down in the box he did go;
   No more Slave work for Henry Box Brown,
   In the box *by Express* he did go.

II.

Then the orders they were given, and the cars did start away;
Roll along—roll along—roll along,
Down to the landing, where the steamboat lay,
To bear the baggage off to the north.
                    CHORUS.

III.

When they packed the baggage on, they turned him on his
      head,
There poor Brown liked to have died;
There were passengers on board who wished to sit down,
And they turned the box down on its side.
                    CHORUS.

IV.

When they got to the cars they threw the box off,
And down upon his head he did fall,
Then he heard his neck crack, and he thought it was broke,
But they never threw him off any more.
                    CHORUS.

When they got to Philadelphia they said he was in port,
And Brown then began to feel glad,
He was taken on the wagon to his final destination,
And left, "this side up with care."

VI.

The friends gathered round and asked if all was right,
As down on the box they did rap,
Brown answered them, saying, "yes all is right!"
He was then set free from his pain.

⊣ APPENDIX ⊢

*The allusion in my song to the shovel and the hoe, is founded on the
following story, which forms the slave-holders' version of the creation
of the human race.*

The slave-holders say that originally, there were four persons created (instead of only two) and, perhaps, it is owing to the christian account of the origin of man, in which account two persons
only are mentioned, that it is one of the doctrines of slave-holders
that slaves have no souls: however, these four persons were two
whites and two blacks; and the blacks were made to wait upon the
whites. But in man's original state when he neither required to
manufacture clothes to cover his nakedness, or to shelter him
from storm; when he did not require to till the earth or to sow or
to reap its fruits, for his support! but when everything sprung up
spontaneously; when the shady bowers invited him to rest, and
the loaded trees dropped their luscious burdens into his hands;
in this state of things the white pair were plagued with the inces-
sant attendance of the two colored persons, and they prayed that
God would find them something else to do; and immediately while
they stood, a black cloud seemed to gather over their heads and

to descend to the earth before them! While they gazed on these clouds, they saw them open and two bags of different size drop from them. They immediately ran to lay hold of the bags, and unfortunately for the black man—he being the strongest and swiftest—he arrived first at them, and laid hold of the bags, and the white man, coming up afterwards, got the smaller one. They then proceeded to untie their bags, when lo! in the large one, there was a shovel and a hoe; and in the small one, a pen, ink, and paper; to write the declaration of the intention of the Almighty; they each proceeded to employ the instruments which God had sent them, and ever since the colored race have had to labor with the shovel and the hoe, while the rich man works with the pen and ink!

I have no apology whatever to make for what I have said, in regard to the pretended christianity under which I was trained, while a slave. I have felt it my duty to speak of it harshly, because I have felt its blasting influence, and seen it used as a cloak under which to conceal the most foul and wicked deeds. Indeed the only thing I think it necessary to say in this place is what seems to me, and what may really be matter of serious doubt to persons who have the privilege of living in a free country, under the influence of liberal institutions; that there actually does exist in that land where men, women, and children are bought and sold, a church, calling itself the church of Christ; yes, my friends, it is true that the buyer and seller of the bodies and souls of his fellows; he who to day, can separate the husband from the wife, the parent from the child, or cut asunder the strongest ties of friendship, in order to gain a few dollars, to avert a trifling loss, or to please a whim of fancy, can ascend a pulpit to-morrow and preach, what he calls, the gospel of Christ! Yes, and in many cases, the house, which he calls the house of God, has been erected from the price of human beings; the very stones of which it is composed, have actually been dragged to their places by men with chains at their heels, and ropes about their neck! It is not for me to judge between those men and the God whom they pretend to serve, if their own consciences do not condemn them. I pray that God may give them light to see the error of their ways, and if they know that they are doing wrongly, that he may give them grace to renovate their hearts!

A few specimens of the laws of a slave-holding people may not be out of place here; not that by such means we can hope to convey a true idea of the actual condition of the people of these places, because those matters on which the happiness or misery of a people principally depend, and in general such matters as are entirely beyond the reach of law. Beside—the various circumstances, which, independent of the law, in civilized and free countries, constitute the principal sources of happiness or misery—in the slave-holding states of America, there is a strong current of public opinion which the law is altogether incompetent to control. In many cases there are ideas of criminality, which are not by statute law attached to the commission of certain acts, but which are frequently found to exist under the title of "Lynch law" either augmenting the punishment which the law requires, or awarding punishment to what the law does not recognize as crime—as the following will be sufficient to show.

"The letter of the law would have been sufficient for the protection of the lives of the miserable gamblers, in Vicksburg, and other places in Mississippi, from the rage of those whose money they had won; but gentlemen of property and standing, laughed the law to scorn, rushed to the gambler's houses, put ropes round their necks, dragged them through the streets, hanged them in the public square, and thus saved the money they had not yet paid. Thousands witnessed this wholesale murder, yet of the scores of legal officers present, not one raised a finger to prevent it. How many hundreds of them helped to commit the murder with their own hands, does not appear, but many of them has been indicted for it, and no one has made the least effort to bring them to trial. Now the laws of Mississippi were not in fault, when those men were murdered, nor were they in fault, that the murderers were not punished; the law demanded it, but the people of Mississippi, the legal officers, the grand juries, and legislature of the state, with one consent determine that the law shall be a dead letter, and thus, the whole state assumes the guilt of these murderers, and, in bravado, flourish their reeking hands in the face of the world; for the people of Vicksburg have actually erected a monument in honor of Dr. H. S. Bodley, who was the ring-leader of the Lynchers in this case." —*American Slavery as it is*.[38]

It may be also worthy of remark, that in all cases in which we have strong manifestation of public opinion, in opposition to the law, it is always exhibited in the direction of cruelty; indeed, that such should be the case, no person intimately acquainted with the nature of the human mind, need be in the least surprised. Who can consider the influence which the relationship of master and slave—so extensively subsisting between the members of slave states—in stimulating the passion and in degrading the moral feelings, without being prepared to credit all that is said of slavery? The most perfect abstract of the laws which regulate the duties of slaves and slave owners, must doubtless fail to convey any proper idea of the actual state of the slave; and the few laws which we here cite, are not given for that purpose, but as a sample of trash, which is called justice by slave-holders and quasi legal authorities.

"All negroes, mulattoes, or mertizoes, who now are, or shall hereafter, be in this province, and all their offspring, are hereby declared to be, and shall remain for ever hereafter, absolute slaves, and shall follow the condition of the mother." —*Law of South Carolina*.

"The criminal offence of assault and battery, cannot, at common law, be committed upon the person of a slave, for, notwithstanding for some purposes, a slave is regarded in law, as a person, yet generally he is a mere chattel personal, and *his right of personal protection belongs to his master*, who can maintain an action of trespass, for the battery of his slave. There can be, therefore, no offence against the state for a mere beating of a slave, unaccompanied by any circumstances of cruelty, or an attempt to kill and murder. The peace of the state, is not thereby broken, for a slave is not generally regarded as legally capable of being within the pale of the State,—HE IS NOT A CITIZEN, AND IS NOT IN THAT CHARACTER ENTITLED TO HER PROTECTION."

"Any person may lawfully kill a slave who has been outlawed for running away and lurking in swamps, &c.,"—*Law of North Carolina*.

"A slave endeavouring to entice another slave to run away, if provision be prepared for the purpose of aiding in such running away, shall be punished with *death*; and a slave who shall aid the slave so endeavouring to run away, shall also suffer *death*."—*Law of South Carolina*.

"If a slave, when absent from his plantation, refuse to be examined by any white person, no matter what the moral character of such white person, or for what purpose he wishes to make the examination, such white person may chastise him, and if, in resisting his chastisement, he should strike the white person, by whom he is being chastised, he may be KILLED."—*Law of South Carolina*.

"If any slave shall presume to strike any white person provided such striking be not done by the command and in defence of the property of the owner, such slave shall, upon trial and conviction, before the justice or justices, suffer such punishment, for the first offence, as they shall think fit, not extending to life or limb, and for the second offence, *death*."—*Law of Georgia*.

"If any person cut any chain or collar, which any master of slaves has put upon his slave, to prevent such slave from running away, such person will be liable to a penalty not exceeding one thousand dollars, and imprisonment not exceeding two years."—*Law of Louisiana*.

"If any person cut out the tongue, put out the eye, cruelly burn, or deprive any slave of a limb, he shall be liable to a penalty not exceeding five hundred dollars."

"If a slave be attacked by any person not having sufficient cause for so doing, and be maimed or disabled so that THE OWNER SUFFERS A LOSS FROM HIS INABILITY TO LABOUR, the person so doing, shall pay the master of such disabled slave, for the time such slave shall be off work, and for the medical attendance on the slave."—*Law of South Carolina*.

If more than seven slaves be found together in any road without a white person, they shall be liable to twenty lashes each.

If any slave visit a plantation, other than that of his master, without a written pass, he shall be liable to ten lashes.

If a slave let loose a boat from where it has been made fast, he shall for the first offence be liable to a penalty of thirty-nine lashes, and for the second, to have one ear cut from his head—for being on horseback, without a written permission from his master—twenty-five lashes; for riding or going abroad at night, without a written permission, a slave may be cropped or branded in the cheek, with the letter E, or otherwise punished, not extending to life, or so as to render him unfit for labour.

HENRY BOX BROWN. FINIS.

Notes

1. From "Forget Not the Unhappy," in Charles Swain's *English Melodies* (1849). Swain (1801-74) included this song, of which the lines Brown quotes are the third and final stanza, in the book's *Part First. Songs and Lyrical Pieces Never Before Published*.

2. The Evangelical Alliance, founded in 1846, was an attempt to organize evangelical churches from around the world. An American delegation attended the first conference in London in 1846, where the British delegation successfully moved to ban slaveholders from membership. As Carwardine has noted, "Evangelical southerners' paranoia and isolation revealed itself in their view of the Evangelical Alliance as an ecclesiastical alliance intending 'to unite the public opinion of Protestant Christendom against the churches and professors of religion in the Southern States'" (*Evangelicals and Politics in Antebellum America*, 384 n. 132).

3. Lee here refers to the story told in the Bible, in the Book of Exodus. Moses leads the Israelites out of slavery in Egypt, across the parted Red Sea, through the wilderness, and toward the promised land. A story of liberation from both slavery and the oppression of an unjust ruler, the Exodus story was one of the central biblical stories of African American writing and oral culture throughout the nineteenth century and since.

4. Ham is a biblical figure often referred to in racial debates throughout the nineteenth century, and Noah's curse on Ham's son Canaan was used as

justification for the enslavement of those of African heritage, who, according to the white supremacist biblical interpretation of the accusers, were said to be the inheritors of the curse of Ham. The curse follows the incident when Ham sees "the nakedness of his father." When Noah awakes from his drunken state, he says, "Cursed be Canaan; a servant of servants shall he be unto his brethren" (Gen. 9:20-27). Canaan's curse was misattributed to Ham and became the foundation for racist readings of the Bible sometime during the Middle Ages. For background, see Byron, *Symbolic Blackness*; Goldenberg, *Curse of Ham*; Hood, *Begrimed and Black*; and Johnson, *Myth of Ham*.

5. Patrick Henry (1736-99) was a Virginia statesman popularly known for his speech before the 1775 Virginia Provincial Convention, in which he said, in support of the American Revolution, "Give me liberty or give me death."

6. This letter was sent to Sydney Howard Gay, a member of the New York Anti-Slavery Society and editor of the influential newspaper the *National Anti-Slavery Standard*.

7. The letter was sent by James Miller McKim (1810-74), a founding member of the American Anti-Slavery Society and, for twenty-five years, corresponding secretary of the Pennsylvania Anti-Slavery Society. McKim was actively involved with the efforts of the General Vigilance Committee of Philadelphia to aid and protect fugitive slaves in the 1850s. McKim was the primary contact in the office of the Pennsylvania Anti-Slavery Society for Brown's escape and made the necessary arrangements for Brown's successful arrival and subsequent safety. Most likely, the name here is changed to protect the Pennsylvania Anti-Slavery Society in its efforts to help fugitive slaves. Note that he leads into the next published letter, in which McKim's name is mentioned, by making it seem as though Brown came to McKim's attention only after "the report of Mr. Brown's escape spread far and wide."

8. The narrative referred to here is the one authored by Charles Stearns in collaboration with Brown, *Narrative of Henry Box Brown, Who Escaped from Slavery Enclosed in a Box 3 Feet Long and 2 Wide. Written from a Statement of Facts Made by Himself, With Remarks Upon the Remedy for Slavery* (1849).

9. Not long after his escape—after he had gained experience on the antislavery stage and presented his first narrative to the public—Brown began planning a moving panorama to dramatize the realities of slavery.

The panorama, *Henry Box Brown's Mirror of Slavery*, was a series of paintings on a long (reported to be 50,000 feet) sheet of canvas that would be gradually unwound to reveal successive representations of scenes related to Brown's personal experience and to the larger history of slavery and the slave trade. Among the numerous titles of the images included were "The Nubian Family in Freedom," "The Seizure of Slaves," "Separation after Sale of Slaves," "Grand Slave Auction," "Sunday among the Slave Population," "Henry Box Brown Released at Philadelphia," "Burning Alive," and "Promise of Freedom," all leading to "Grand Tableau Finale, Universal Emancipation." Advertisements for the panorama promised as well "vocal and instrumental music to accompany exhibition." Brown toured with the panorama initially in the United States and later in England, with the help of his friend James C. A. Smith. Eventually, tensions in that friendship broke up the collaborative performance. Brown would later tour in England with his wife and the panorama, now titled *Grand Original Panorama of African and American Slavery*.

10. Probably the Reverend Justin Spaulding, a Methodist minister and missionary.

11. Probably the Reverend Alanson Latham, a Methodist minister.

12. The Reverend Arthur Caverno (1801–76) was an active and influential Baptist minister of New Hampshire. Converted to the Free Will Baptist Faith when he was seventeen, Caverno served as pastor at various churches in New Hampshire, Massachusetts, and Maine throughout his long career and was a frequent contributor to the *Morning Star*, a denominational paper.

13. Samuel J. May (1810–99) was a Unitarian clergyman who served as the general agent of the Massachusetts Anti-Slavery Society from 1847 to 1865.

14. The Reverend Thomas Gardiner Lee was active in reform movements and pastor of the New Windsor Independent Chapel of Salford, close to Manchester, where the *Narrative* was published. Lee was committed to a number of causes, including temperance and the elevation of working classes.

15. From Bernard Barton's "A Child's Dream," in *Household Verses* (1845). Barton (1784–1849) was a poet known in British antislavery circles and contributed "Introductory Poem" to British abolitionist Wilson Armistead's important 1848 collection of biographical narratives and historical

sketches, *A Tribute for the Negro: Being a Vindication of the Moral, Intellectual, and Religious Capabilities of the Coloured Portion of Mankind; with Particular Reference to the African Race.*

16. The lines Brown quotes here come from a variety of sources. The first four lines are a revision of lines from Psalm LI of *The Psalms* (1765), by James Merrick (1720–69). Merrick's version reads,

O turn, great Ruler of the Skies,
Turn from my Sin thy searching eyes,
Nor let th'offences of my hand
Within thy book recorded stand.

Changing "my Sin" to "their sins," and "my hand" to "their hands," Brown points divine judgment toward the many involved in the collective sin of slavery.

The next four lines come from Isaac Watts's "Hymn 99" from vol. 4 of Watts's *Works* (1810), *Hymns and Spiritual Songs, in Three Books. Book II. Composed on Divine Subjects.* Watts (1674–1748) was one of the most important and influential writers of hymns.

The last four lines in this quotation remain unidentified.

17. Barret did not have a son named "Stronn." Ruggles speculates that this "is undoubtedly the amanuensis's rendering of Brown's spoken pronunciation of Strachan, the maiden name of John Barret's wife and the middle name of two of Barret's sons" (*Unboxing*, 129).

18. Nat Turner's insurrection in Southampton, Virginia (August 21–23), was probably the most famous of the slave revolts and was often mentioned in antislavery and African American orations and publications.

19. From the Bible, Prov. 28:1: "The wicked flee when no man pursueth: but the righteous are bold as a lion." It is useful also to read the lines that follow: "For the transgression of a land many are the princes thereof: but by a man of understanding and knowledge the state thereof shall be prolonged. A poor man that oppresseth the poor is like a sweeping rain which leaveth no food. They that forsake the law praise the wicked: but such as keep the law contend with them. Evil men understand not judgment: but they that seek the Lord understand all things" (Prov. 28:2–5).

20. After the American Revolution, the Church of England, or Anglican Church, was transformed into the Protestant Episcopal Church, which preserved many of the forms of worship and principles of institutional

organization practiced in the Church of England and remains within the Anglican Communion in its historical ties and in the honor it grants to the archbishop of Canterbury. "Episcopalian," from the Greek *episkopos* (roughly, "overseer"), refers to the centrality of bishops in providing theological and ancestral continuity and unity to the churches as well as institutional leadership.

21. Brown refers here to Elder Jacob Knapp (1799-1874), a famous and sometimes controversial Baptist evangelist devoted to revivalism and religious reform. According to Smith, "Knapp's ministry in the 1830's was principally to rural and small-town communities in New York, where he became known as a chief supporter of Madison University at Hamilton. His first urban successes, in union campaigns sponsored by the Baptist churches in Rochester, Baltimore, and Boston, were cut short in 1842 when antirevival clergymen charged that he wore old clothes in the pulpit in order to secure a more sympathetic response in the offerings. His supporters hotly contested the accusation, and he was officially cleared" (*Revivalism & Social Reform*, 47).

Elder Knapp discusses his visit to Richmond in the *Autobiography of Elder Jacob Knapp* (1868), noting that the people who invited him asked him to "give them a pledge" that he "would keep silence on the subject of slavery" (153). Knapp refused to make such a pledge but was invited anyway, and his description of his increasingly tense visit (during which he spoke on a number of occasions) is instructive:

> While I was there a band of colored brethren and sisters, moved by the Spirit of God, met together in order to sing praises and unite in supplication to the Lord. They were surprised by a set of devils (called offers of the peace!), and those who could not escape were dragged to the whipping-post, and lashed to laceration, for no other offence than daring to meet without the presence of a white man. Throughout the night the slave-hounds were on the scent for these victims, and the hours were made hideous with their howlings. It seemed as if I was in Pandemonium. (Knapp, *Autobiography*, 155)

Knapp's increasing anger at the white slaveholding population—he wonders, "How could I ask God to hear the prayers of such a people?"—led him to be more direct in his comments on slavery and to "preach, with increasing plainness, the Bible doctrines concerning human rights, and those which cut up this system root and branch." Finally, Knapp reports, "I was visited by a committee, and requested to preach no more, unless I would promise to keep silent on the subject of slavery" (155–56). Knapp refused to make such a promise and was therefore forced to leave the area.

22. From the Bible, Matt. 23:37 and Luke 13:34. This passage comes at the end of an angry complaint by Jesus against the religious leaders who opposed him. The refrain that runs through these two books is "Woe unto you, scribes and Pharisees, hypocrites." Significantly for Knapp's visit to the South, considering the troubles he encountered there, Jesus admonishes "the multitude" and his disciples, "Wherefore, behold, I send unto you prophets, and wise men, and scribes; and *some* of them ye shall kill and crucify; and *some* of them shall ye scourge in your synagogues, and persecute *them* from city to city" (Matt. 23:34). Significantly, too, the chapter ends, "For I say unto you, Ye shall not see me henceforth, till ye shall say, Blessed *is* he that cometh in the name of the Lord" (Matt. 23:39).

23. The phrase "tender mercies" appears numerous times in the Psalms in the Bible, notably in Psalm 40, the source of the hymn that Brown sang after he stepped out of the box following his safe arrival in Philadelphia.

24. On the Reverend Robert Ryland and the First African Baptist Church of Richmond, see n. 17 in my Introduction.

25. From the Bible, Eph. 6:5–8: "Servants, be obedient to them that are our masters according to the flesh, with fear and trembling, in singleness of your heart, as unto Christ; Not with eyeservice, as menpleasers; but as the servants of Christ, doing the will of God from the heart; With good will doing service, as to the Lord, and not to men: Knowing that whatsoever good thing any man doeth, the same shall he receive of the Lord, whether he be bond or free." A similar message appears in Luke 12:47: "And that servant, which knew his lord's will, and prepared not himself, neither did according to his will, shall be beaten with many stripes."

A number of publications by former slaves testify to the prominence given to these and similar passages as part of the biblical defense of slavery and as part of the efforts by slaveholders and proslavery preachers to use religion as one of many means by which to shape and control the slave population. Episcopal bishop William Meade of Virginia edited a collection of sermons of this type in 1813, *Sermons Addressed to Masters and Servants, and Published in the Year 1743, by the Rev. Thomas Bacon, Minister of the Protestant Episcopal Church in Maryland. Now Republished with other Tracts and Dialogues on the Same Subject, and Recommended to all Masters and Mistresses to be Used in Their Families.*

26. James Caesar Anthony Smith was a free black man in Richmond, where both he and Brown sang in the church choir. Reportedly, he had been a dentist at one point, which is why Brown sometimes refers to him as Doctor Smith, and was the proprietor of a cake shop when he and Brown were friends. Smith was Brown's confidant when Brown prepared to escape, and after helping Brown, Smith contributed to additional but unsuccessful efforts. After being arrested twice in Richmond, Smith moved north and soon joined Brown, after which the two collaborated on the creation and public presentation of Brown's panorama, *Mirror of Slavery*. For his contribution to Brown's escape, Smith was given the nickname James Boxer Smith by the abolitionist Samuel Ringgold Ward at the 1849 meeting of the "Anti-Slavery Mass Convention, of the Abolitionists of the State of New York" in Syracuse.

27. From the Bible, wherein Jesus is asked by the Pharisees about marriage. "The Pharisees also came unto him, tempting him, and saying unto him, Is it lawful for a man to put away his wife for every cause?" (Matt. 19:3): "What therefore God hath joined together, let not man put asunder" (Matt. 19:6). The verse is regularly quoted in religious wedding ceremonies.

28. From William Mason's "Hymn Before Morning Service," included in Mason's *Works*, vol. 1, *Hymns and Select Psalms Versified* (1811). Mason (1725–97) was a British poet known for his association with the poet Thomas Gray as well as for such works of his own as the tragedy *Elfrida* and the long blank-verse poem *The English Garden*.

29. These lines are from Alexander Pope's "The Dying Christian to His Soul, Ode," from Pope's *Works* (1736), vol. 1, *Ode on Cecilia's Day, 1708. And Other Pieces for Music.* Pope (1688–1744), the son of a Roman Catholic linen-draper of London, England, is widely considered one of the great poets in the English language and has certainly been one of the most influential. The first stanza of "The Dying Christian to His Soul" reads as follows:

Vital spark of heav'nly flame!
Quit, oh quit this mortal frame:
Trembling, hoping, ling'ring, flying,

Oh the pain, the bliss of dying!
Cease, fond Nature, cease thy strife,
And let me languish into life.

"The Dying Christian to His Soul" was used as a hymn—and this is the probable source of Brown's encounter with these lines. The hymn appears in the *Southern Harmony* by William Walker. First published in 1835, and with editions extending to 1854, Walker's *Southern Harmony* was an influential collection of hymns, including folk hymns, rendered in "shape-note" format, a presentation of music designed to simplify reading for congregations unschooled in music notation. The hymn's opening lines appear in the *Southern Harmony* as follows:

Vital spark of heavenly flame,
Quit, O quit this mortal frame;
Trembling, hoping, lingering,
Flying flying flying,
O the pain, the bliss of dying!
Cease, fond nature, cease thy strife,
And let me languish into life;
And let me languish into life.

Worth noting, too, is Josiah Conder's *The Dying Christian. A Parody*, which appeared in Conder's *The Choir and The Oratory* (1837). Conder (1789-1855) was a British writer; the opening stanza of his "parody" of Pope's poem/hymn reads as follows:

"Vital spark of heavenly flame!"
Thou must quit this mortal frame.
Yet on Christ, this life, relying,
Death is gain; then fear not dying.
Soon shall cease this mortal strife,
And death be swallowed up of life.

30. Brown here refers to Samuel Alexander Smith, who helped him escape. Originally from Massachusetts, Smith was the proprietor of a shoe store in Richmond when Brown approached him. Smith had owned slaves at least until 1846, so he was hardly an antislavery advocate hidden in the South—though he did claim in later years that he had been involved in

the Underground Railroad for decades before he helped Brown. In any event, a significant motive for helping Brown was financial, since Brown offered to pay him for his assistance. Smith's personal and business habits had placed him in a discomforting financial condition. Whatever his motives, Smith was essential to Brown's escape, contacting the Philadelphia antislavery agents and making the necessary arrangements for Brown's reception. When Smith tried to send two other fugitives to Philadelphia by the same means, however, he was arrested, convicted of both charges, and sent to "the Virginia State Penitentiary in Richmond to serve consecutive sentences totaling six and a half years" (Ruggles, *Unboxing*, 67). He was released in 1856, after which he moved to the North, where he was honored at a meeting held by "the colored citizens of Philadelphia" (ibid., 161).

31. Sulfuric acid.

32. Brown drew this hymn from the Psalms in the Bible. The first three verses of Psalm 40 read as follows: "I waited patiently for the Lord; and he inclined unto me, and heard my cry. He brought me up also out of a horrible pit, out of the miry clay, and set my feet upon a rock, and established my goings. And he hath put a new song in my mouth, even praise unto our God: many shall see it, and fear, and shall trust in the Lord."

William Still, the great black abolitionist who served as secretary and executive director of the General Vigilance Committee in Philadelphia, was present for Brown's arrival and reports the following on Brown's presentation of this hymn: "Very soon he remarked that, before leaving Richmond he had selected for his arrival-hymn (if he lived) the Psalm beginning with these words: '*I waited patiently for the Lord, and He heard my prayer.*' And most touchingly did he sing the psalm, much to his own relief, as well as to the delight of his small audience" (Still, *Underground Rail Road*, 70). Still's account is reprinted in Appendix B.

33. Brown stayed with prominent abolitionists James and Lucretia Mott. The Motts were active in various reform efforts, and the Quaker minister Lucretia Mott (1793–1880) in particular was an important antislavery activist and early leader of the Philadelphia Female Anti-Slavery Society. In 1840 Mott went to the World Anti-Slavery Convention in London and, although she attended as a delegate, was denied a seat because of her gender. Mott formed alliances between the antislavery and the women's movements, working with and influencing Elizabeth Cady Stanton and others

over the years, and she was one of the organizers of the women's rights meeting at Seneca Falls in 1848.

34. Edward M. Davis was a member of the Executive Committee of the Pennsylvania Anti-Slavery Society and the son-in-law of James and Lucretia Mott. Davis, deeply engaged in business and familiar with the Adams Express (the service used to ship Brown), was able to help arrange for Brown's safe arrival in Philadelphia without arousing suspicion.

35. Possibly H. Long of the publisher H. Long and Brother, which published a variety of books, from narratives and fiction concerning slavery to collections of minstrel songs.

36. On 29 March 1849 Brown was actually received in New Bedford, Massachusetts, not by H. Ricketson but by Joseph Ricketson Jr., called by one scholar "probably the most committed white abolitionist the city ever produced" (Grover, *Fugitive's Gibraltar*, 6). Ricketson wrote to James Miller McKim, "I received your very valuable consignment of 200 pounds of Humanity last evening and as merchants say will dispose of it to the best advantage." Ricketson noted as well that Brown's sister was also in New Bedford, though her presence there has not been verified by scholars, and that Brown had "many friends here [in New Bedford] who former [sic] lived in Richmond" (qtd. in ibid., 202).

37. "Uncle Ned," also known as "Old Uncle Ned," is a minstrel song by Stephen Foster (1826-64). Blackface minstrelsy was at this time one of the most popular forms of entertainment in the United States and would remain so for quite some time. Minstrel shows featured white performers who would blacken their faces and perform exaggerated caricatures of what white Americans imagined to be the features of African American identity and folk culture. Henry Box Brown, then, is taking a racist form of entertainment and transforming a song about the death of a slave into a story of escape, perhaps in this way signaling his resistance not only to slavery but also to white racist culture. Some of the lyrics to "Uncle Ned," as noted by Emerson in his study of Stephen Foster's influence on American popular culture, are as follows:

Dere was an old Nigga, dey call'd him Uncle Ned
He's dead long ago, long ago!
He had no wool on de top ob his head
De place whar de wool ought to grow.

Den lay down de shubble and de hoe
Hang up de fiddle and de bow
No more hard work for poor old Ned
He's gone whar de good Niggas go.

For commentary and background on this and other songs by Stephen Foster, see Emerson, *Doo-Dah!*

38. A reference to *American Slavery As It Is*, by Theodore Weld, a compilation of narratives, "testimonies" by white southerners, articles from southern papers, and other forms of evidence concerning the physical violence and other abuses common in the slave system. The evidence was gathered by Weld, his wife Angelina Grimké Weld, and Angelina's sister Sarah Grimké. Published in 1839, *American Slavery As It Is* provided material for a number of subsequent antislavery writers and was one of the most influential of all antislavery publications.

APPENDIX A

ILLUSTRATIONS

Included in the title of Brown's first narrative, published in the same year of his escape, were the rough dimensions of the box in which he traveled from Richmond to Philadelphia: "a Box 3 Feet Long and 2 Wide." Mentioned regularly in the many press notices that followed his escape, and in remarks about Brown in speeches by other abolitionists, were more precise measurements: "exactly *three feet one inch long, two feet wide, and two feet six inches deep.*" Brown's daring escape seemed so sensational that many spectators were naturally eager to see the box itself, and Brown would sometimes satisfy their curiosity by displaying the box during his public appearances. Audiences also enjoyed the songs Brown performed at those appearances, one of which was the song he sang shortly after he emerged from the box following his safe arrival in Philadelphia. It is hardly surprising, then, that published song sheets and visual images soon played a significant role in Brown's developing fame.

Included in this appendix and elsewhere in this edition of Brown's *Narrative* is a sampling of the images and song sheets that tell the story of Brown's journey. Shortly after Brown's escape—probably in June 1849—a song sheet was printed that offered the lyrics of the hymn Brown famously sang in the office of the Pennsylvania Anti-Slavery Society in Philadelphia. Included on the song sheet was a woodcut representation of the box itself, reprinted below. Another song sheet, also reprinted below, and with the same representation of the box, was published about that same time, though this version included the lyrics of Brown's other famous song—his rewriting of Stephen Foster's minstrel tune "Old Uncle Ned"—in which Brown tells the story of his escape. Such illustrated song sheets were popular at the time, and many antislavery song sheets and songbooks were published, widely circulated, and probably used at antislavery events when either those on the stage or those in the hall would sing sometimes somber and sometimes satiric songs about slavery, always leading to a determined chorus of resistance.

Soon, readers and audiences were introduced to the man hidden in the box. Brown's first narrative drew from the already published representations of his box, reprinting the image of the box and adding a testimonial to the significance of Brown's bold escape. The narrative included as well an image of Brown himself, comfortably seated in a chair and dignified in demeanor and dress. Other images focused on what many viewed as the most significant, the most emotionally compelling, moment of Brown's story: his emergence from the box while surrounded by Philadelphia abolitionists. The first representation of Brown's emergence from the box was published shortly after his escape, in a children's book titled *Cousin Ann's Stories for Children*. The book was published by James Miller McKim, who was instrumental in helping Brown in his escape and who was present when Brown emerged from the box. That image, and the story that it illustrates—including McKim's care to have the box inaccurately addressed to "Thomas Wilson" so as not to expose the Philadelphia activists who assisted Brown—is included with the text from *Cousin Ann's Stories* in Appendix B. That first image is only a rough representation, but other representations quickly followed. Two of the handful of prints or sketches inspired by the story of Brown's emergence are reproduced below. Another, slightly different version of this image was used as the frontispiece of Brown's 1851 *Narrative*, and it is reproduced at the beginning of the *Narrative* in this edition as well.

As his subsequent career with the various versions of his panorama makes clear, Brown understood the value of visual representations. His was a story that inspired and provoked the imagination, leading the mind's eye to re-create unimaginable pain and striking determination in the form of a box, and spiritual jubilation and political resistance in an office scene, with a box newly opened and a man just emerging into his new life of freedom. The images below, at the beginning of the *Narrative*, and in

Cousin's Ann's Stories for Children are included to give readers, no doubt engaged in their own imaginative re-creations, an opportunity to see Brown's emerging presence in antislavery culture.

For the most comprehensive collection of images and advertisements related to Brown's narratives, his panorama, and his public career generally, see Jeffrey Ruggles's *The Unboxing of Henry Brown*. Ruggles offers the most detailed and authoritative commentary on these images, and I am indebted to him for much of the information included in this appendix.

**Engraving of the Box in which HENRY BOX
BROWN escaped from slavery in Richmond, Va.**

SONG,

Sung by Mr. Brown on being removed from the box.

I waited patiently for the Lord ;—
And he, in kindness to me, heard my calling—
And he hath put a new song into my mouth—
Even thanksgiving—even thanksgiving—
  Unto our God !

Blessed—blessed is the man
That has set his hope, his hope in the Lord !
O Lord ! my God ! great, great is the wondrous work
  Which thou hast done !

If I should declare them—and speak of them—
They would be more than I am able to express.
I have not kept back thy love, and kindness, and truth,
  From the great congregation !

Withdraw not thou thy mercies from me,
Let thy love, and kindness, and thy truth, alway preserve me—
Let all those that seek thee be joyful and glad !
  Be joyful and glad !

And let such as love thy salvation—
Say always—say always—
The Lord be praised !
  The Lord be praised !

Laing's Steam Press, 1 1-3 Water Street, Boston.

25/089
14

*Engraving of the Box in which Henry Box Brown escaped from
slavery in Richmond, Va.* Laing's Steam Press, Boston, ca. June 1849.
Courtesy of the Library of Congress, Rare Book and
Special Collections Division.

The origins of this engraving are unknown, though probably the intention was that Brown could sell it for income while also promoting the antislavery cause. The lyrics, drawn from Psalm 40, are of the hymn Brown sang following his safe arrival—his resurrection, as many called it—in Philadelphia. In the various versions of Brown's story that appeared in the press, and in his *Narrative* itself, the box is said to have been marked "This side up with care." The box presented here, though, is marked "Right side up with care." What might be the *right* side is unclear, but the lettering is facing the viewer, so the box might well be on its side. Of course, the inscription on the box, like the abbreviated address (only "Philadelphia, Pa."), is not intended to be an accurate representation. Rather, it suggests the box's dimensions, indicating the courage it would take to submit oneself to that box for well over twenty-four hours.

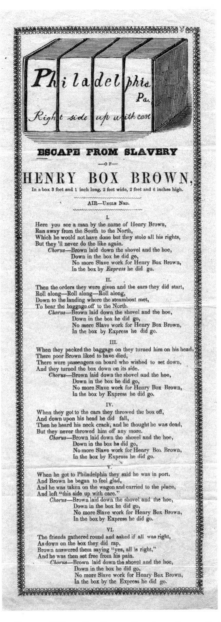

Escape from Slavery of Henry Box Brown, In a box 3 feet and 1 inch long, 2 feet wide, 2 feet and 6 inches high. Broadside. Boston, ca. June or July 1849. Courtesy of the American Antiquarian Society.

The origins of this broadside are unknown, but it was available for those familiar with Brown's public appearances. The image of the box is the same one used in the preceding image, this time accompanied by Brown's rewriting of "Old Uncle Ned." Brown plays especially with the line "Den lay down de shubble and de hoe," which becomes "Brown laid down the shovel and the hoe," the first step of his escape. Brown would soon construct a story about the shovel and the hoe that he related regularly in his public appearances, a story included in his 1851 *Narrative*.

Henry Box Brown. Frontispiece of *Narrative of Henry Box Brown, Who Escaped from Slavery Enclosed in a Box 3 Feet Long and 2 Wide. Written from a Statement of Facts Made by Himself, With Remarks Upon the Remedy for Slavery* (Boston: Brown & Stearns, 1849). Courtesy of the Rare Books, Manuscripts, and Special Collections Library, Duke University.

The source of this engraving is unclear, but it was said by Brown's contemporaries to be a good likeness. It is interesting to note that this same image would reappear in 1854 depicting a different fugitive slave, Anthony Burns. This recirculation of images was common in the antislavery movement, and sometimes startling. By placing existing sketches and prints in dramatically different contexts, authors, printers, and publishers turned British abolitionists into American slaveholders, used the image of one African American to represent another, and turned proslavery images into antislavery messages. The best commentary on such recycled images is in Marcus Wood's *Blind Memory*.

Representation of the Box. Last page of *Narrative of Henry Box Brown,*
Who Escaped from Slavery Enclosed in a Box 3 Feet Long and 2 Wide. Written from
a Statement of Facts Made by Himself, With Remarks Upon the Remedy for Slavery
(Boston: Brown & Stearns, 1849). Courtesy of the Rare Books, Manuscripts,
and Special Collections Library, Duke University.

The same representation of the box circulated in Brown's song sheets, published in June or July 1849, was reproduced in his first narrative, published in September of that year. The box is still marked "Right side up with care," but now the image itself is turned on its side—with a caption to the right for those who want to see it as it appeared in the song sheets, and with text above and below that encourages one as well to see the box sitting on end. Given Brown's tumbling during shipment, in which his box was sometimes placed wrong side up and with little care, this representation is quietly and perhaps inadvertently appropriate as a representation not only of the box but of its journey.

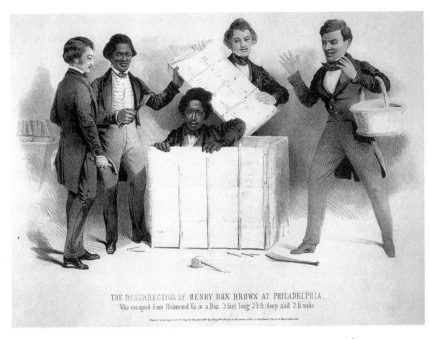

THE RESURRECTION OF HENRY BOX BROWN AT PHILADELPHIA.
Who escaped from Richmond Va. in a Box. 3 feet long 2½ ft. deep and 2 ft wide

The Resurrection of Henry Box Brown at Philadelphia, Who escaped from Richmond Va. in a Box 3 feet long 2½ ft. deep and 2 ft. wide. Lithograph. Deposited for copyright in Boston on January 10, 1850. Courtesy of the Library of Congress, Prints and Photographs Division, LC-USZ62-1283.

Although this print is not signed, scholars generally agree that it is the work of Samuel Worcester Rowse (1822-1901), a well-known artist who also produced drawings of such well-known figures as Ralph Waldo Emerson, Henry David Thoreau, and Nathaniel Hawthorne. This image represents Brown in the moment after the box's lid was removed. To Brown's right is James Miller McKim, who played a prominent role in Brown's escape. The two other white figures are intended to represent Lewis Thompson and Charles D. Cleveland, though the images were likely based on other men. Similarly, the black man portrayed here seems to be based on Frederick Douglass, though it is meant as a representation of William Still. Faintly, one can see that Rowse was attentive in marking the box "This side up with care" and in placing that side up. This image was the source for the frontispiece, reproduced in this edition, of Brown's 1851 *Narrative*.

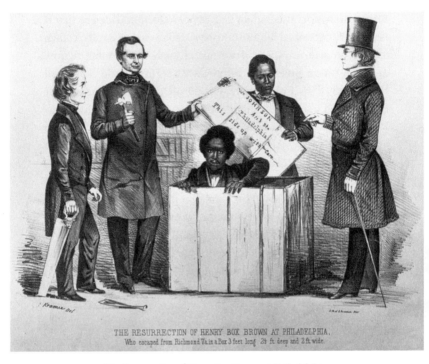

THE RESURRECTION OF HENRY BOX BROWN AT PHILADELPHIA,
Who escaped from Richmond Va. in a Box 3 feet long 2½ ft. deep and 2 ft. wide.

The Resurrection of Henry Box Brown at Philadelphia,
Who escaped from Richmond Va. in a Box 3 feet long 2½ ft. deep and 2 ft. wide.
Lithograph by Peter Kramer. Philadelphia, ca. 1851.
Courtesy of the Library Company of Philadelphia.

Published in early 1851, this representation is by Peter Kramer (1823-1907), a painter and lithographer who had emigrated from Bavaria to the United States in 1848. Kramer followed the basic design of Samuel Rowse's print, but Kramer lived in Philadelphia and was able to base his representations on the actual people at attendance during Brown's emergence from the box. Lewis Thompson stands at the far left, with James Miller McKim next to him. To the right are William Still and Charles D. Cleveland. In this print, too, the box itself is more accurately represented, for it includes the name and address that appeared on the box, along with the instructions "This side up with care."

Brown's daring escape made him an immediate celebrity in anti-slavery circles and beyond. The following collection focuses primarily on early notices of Brown and early versions of Brown's story. One can see in these notices the rising fame of Brown's story as well as details that became standard parts of the story. One can also see how Brown's story was placed in the service of the antislavery movement. Included here are private as well as public versions of Brown's story, accounts of the antislavery convention where Brown was introduced to the public, other newspaper notices of Brown's activities and fame, reviews of his first published narrative, and a poem and a children's story based on his experience. Almost all of these pieces focus on Brown's early antislavery career, before his move to England. The one later piece is William Still's account of Brown's escape in *The Underground Rail Road* (1872), included here because Still was a witness to Brown's arrival in Philadelphia. For an overview of Brown's reception in England, see the introduction to this edition and Appendix C, which compares the 1849 and 1851 narratives.

⊰ ⊱

From the diary of Charles Waln Morgan,[1] April 4, 1849, quoted in Grover, *Fugitive's Gibraltar*, 203.

Sarah & I went to Wm J Rotchs[2] to tea but came home early—I there heard a singular account of the escape of a slave who has just arrived here which I must record—He had himself packed up in a box about 3 ft 2 in long 2 ft 6 in wide & 1 ft 11 in deep and sent on by express from Richmond to Philadelphia—marked "this side up"—He is about 5 ft 6 in high and weighs about 200 lb—In this way he came by cars & steam boat to Philada near 25 hours in the box which was quite close & tight had only a bladder of water with him and kept himself alive by bathing his face and fanning himself with his hat. He was twice turned head downwards & once remained so on board the steam boat while she went 18 miles — which almost killed him and he said the veins on his temples were almost as thick as his finger. Yet he endured it all and was delivered to his antislavery friends safe & well — who trembled when he knocked on the box and asked the question "all right["] — and the answer came promptly "all right sir" — I think I never heard of an instance of greater fortitude & daring and he has well earned the freedom which he will now enjoy —

⊰ ⊱

The Liberator, April 20, 1849

Another Wonderful Escape.

The Burlington (Vt.) Courier of the 12th instant[3] tells the following story. What an item to be circulated by every European journal!

A few weeks ago, a slave in a Southern city managed to open a correspondence with a gentleman in a Northern city, with a view of effecting an escape from bondage. Having arranged the preliminaries, he paid somebody $40 to box him up, and mark him "This side up with care," and take him to the express office, consigned to his friend at the North. On the passage, being on board of a steamboat, he was accidentally turned head downwards, and almost died with the rush of blood to the head. At the next change of transportation, however, he was turned right side up again, and after twenty-six hours' confinement, arrived safely at his destination. On receiving the box, the gentleman had his doubts whether he should find a corpse or a free man. He tapped lightly on the box, with the question "All right?" and was delighted to hear the response, "All right, sir." The poor fellow was immediately liberated from his place of living burial, and forwarded to a wealthy Abolitionist in a city in New England, where he now is. When did Spartan intrepidity show greater firmness and fortitude under bodily suffering, than did this poor slave when animated by the inspiring hope of freedom?[4] We are glad to have assurance that this story is no flight of fancy, but is absolutely true. The fugitive, upon whose track the two-legged blood-hounds are coursing, will never go back to slavery, if the whole South should come after him.

⤙ ⤚

From a letter, Joseph Ricketson Jr. to Debora Weston,[5] April 29, 1849, quoted in Grover, *Fugitive's Gibraltar*, 203.

The man appears to be a fine fellow, has found considerable employment—he has worked several days for me & if I commence manufacturing oil again I think I can give him constant employment. Noble as was the sentiment uttered by Patrick Henry, "Give [me] liberty or give me Death," how much nobler and more difficult was the carrying out of the spirit of the sentiment in the case of this man. Every one that hears of it or seen him are astonished. They all glorify in it & I think it will have a strong tendency to cement the Anti Slavery feeling here. Only one man, and he an exdivine of the Orthodox School, Pardon G. Seabury, doubted the veracity of the story as Mr. Robeson informed me, but he no longer doubts, for as we were standing at the Post Office last Friday, the man came along and I informed him Mr. Seabury of it; it was "prima facie"[6] evidence. Orthodoxy stood abashed; God's image in an ebony case confronted it too strongly; what says he? you dont mean "that nigger", yes, says I, there is the Hero; such I'll give up says he were it not for *exposing* the *express* I would call a town meeting and show him up. His name is Henry Brown and he is the greatest Lion of the age—

⤙ ⤚

New England Evangelist, June 7, 1849

The New-England Anti-Slavery Society.

This Society was organized for a three days' meeting Tuesday morning at the Melodeon,[7] Wendell Phillips[8] in the chair. Soon after the opening of the meeting, the Secretary read a series of resolutions which should serve as a foundation for the discussions which might arise during the progress of the meeting. On[e] motion, one which recommended the immediate dissolution of the free States from the slave States, was selected as the first for discussion.

At one of these meetings, Brown, the fugitive slave, whose extraordinary escape from servitude in Richmond, and almost miraculous arrival at Philadelphia, created such a sensation about two weeks since, was introduced to the audience. He was actually transported three hundred miles through a slaveholding country and by public thoroughfares, in a box, by measurement, exactly *three feet one inch long, two feet wide, and two feet six inches deep.* Brown, for that is his name now, told his story in an artless manner, and with natural diffidence. He is of course unlettered, but his adventures and the fortitude with which he bore the perils and privations of his terrible journey, excited, says the Boston Traveller, a thrill of sympathy and admiration in every one who listened. The following is an abstract of his story:

While at Richmond, though the box was legibly and distinctly marked, "this side up with care," it was placed on end, with his head downwards. He felt strange pains, and was preparing himself to die, preferring liberty or death to slavery, and he gave no sign. He was however relieved from this painful position, and encountered no other danger than the rough handling of the box, until it arrived at Washington. When the porters who had charge of it reached the depot there, they threw or dropped it with violence to the ground, and it rolled down a small hill, turning over two or three times. This he thought was bad enough, but the words he heard, filled him with anguish, and brought with them the blackness of despair. They were, that the box was so heavy it could not be forwarded that night, but must lay over twenty-four hours. In the language of the fugitive, "My heart swelled in my throat; I could scarcely breathe; great sweats came over me; I gave up all hope. But it was put into my remembrance that the preacher had said, it is good to pray at all times. So I tried to pray: 'Lord Jesus, put it into the hearts of these men to find a way to send this box forward.' While I was yet praying, a man came in and said, 'that box must go on; it's the express mail.' Oh, what relief I felt. It was taken into the depot, and I was placed head downwards again for the space of half an hour. My eyes were swollen almost out of my head, and I was fast becoming insensible, when the position was changed."

He arrived at Philadelphia after many hair-breadth escapes, and the box was taken to the house to which it was directed. The panting inmate heard voices whispering; afterwards more men came in. They were doubtful or fearful about opening the box. He lay still, not knowing who the people were. Finally, one of them knocked on the box, and asked, "Is all right here?" "All right," echoed from the box. The finale of this simple tale was received with deafening shouts.

In corroboration of it, Rev. S. J. May said he was in Philadelphia in the midst of the excitement caused by this wonderful adventure. He said that, for obvious reasons, he could not give the name of the gentleman to whom the box was consigned, but he knew him as a warm-hearted friend of humanity. That gentleman had told him, Mr. M., that when the box arrived at his house, he was overcome with agitation. The man might be dead. He hoped, yet feared. It might be necessary to call a coroner. He finally assembled several true friends, and then tremblingly asked, "Is all right here?" The voice came up, as if from the grave, "All right." The reaction of his feelings was so great as to stop his breath; but when he could speak, he wildly exclaimed, "You are the greatest man in America."

The fugitive when released, after stretching his limbs, did not appear fatigued. The glorious sense of freedom was upon him in his heart, pervading his whole being, and burst out into song. This was the appropriate anthem of deliverance:

"I waited patiently, and the Lord hath delivered me."

Such, concluded Mr. May, is the man who hath been added to the freemen of the North. Shall we not receive him as a brother beloved? [Loud huzzas responded to this question.]

Frederick Douglass[9] introduced two other fugitive slaves,

William and Ellen Crafts [*sic*].[10] William Crafts stated the manner of their escape from slavery, which was full of adventure and romantic interest. In *four* and a half days, they escaped from Georgia to Philadelphia, a distance of upwards of *one thousand miles*. Crafts and his wife belonged to different masters. He was a cabinet-maker and hired his time for $220 per year; this gave him more liberty than is usually allotted to slaves. She was a lady's maid. They met at nights only, and for weeks pondered over and perfected their scheme.

It was determined that she, being almost white, with straight hair, should disguise herself as an invalid young man, and take the husband as her servant. Their plan succeeded, and they are free! Such indomitable courage and perseverance betoken, on the part of Ellen, a mind of no common energy. The appearance of these fugitives upon the platform, created a deep sensation.

"What an exhibition!" exclaimed Frederick Douglass, triumphantly, himself a fugitive slave.[11] "What an appearance is here presented! Are the slaves contented and happy? Here are three facts—aye, four—that sweep away all the sophistry of Calhoun,[12] McDuffie,[13] and other stout defenders of the patriarchal institution. Their escape shows that they are worthy to be freemen."

Henry *Box* Brown was requested to sing the anthem with which he celebrated his first minute of freedom. He sang amid profound stillness, but when he concluded, the air was rent with loud applause.

-≼ ≽-

The Liberator, June 8, 1849

New England Anti-Slavery Convention

[selected excerpts]

TUESDAY

Edmund Quincy,[14] by request of the Business Committee, offered, and in an eloquent speech sustained the following resolution:—

RESOLVED, That it is our duty to agitate the question of slavery till the soil of New England is pure enough to free every man who sets foot upon it; and meanwhile, we pledge ourselves to trample under foot any law which allows the slaveholder to hunt the fugitive slave through our borders, and not only to make New England, so far as in us lies, an asylum for the oppressed, but to proclaim the fact so loudly that the glad tidings may reach every slave hut of the South.

The resolution was also ably supported by Wm. W. Brown,[15] who then introduced to the audience Wm. and Ellen Craft, who recently made their escape from slavery by the wife personating the master, while the husband acted the part of a servant. He also introduced Henry Brown, who procured his freedom by causing himself to be enclosed in a box, three feet and one inch long, two feet wide, and two feet and six inches deep, and thus transported by express from Richmond to Philadelphia. At this time, *six* fugitive slaves were standing together on the platform.

WEDNESDAY

William W. Brown, himself a fugitive slave, asked permission to introduce to the audience Henry Brown, the slave who, to effect his escape, came from Richmond Virginia to Philadelphia in a box, wherein he was confined for the space of twenty-seven hours.

Henry Brown then came forward, and gave a brief, simple but very interesting account of his escape, and of the circumstances which led to it. After which, Wendell Phillips proposed a collection in the audience in behalf of Henry Brown, as he had been wronged out of the whole of his money (which he left in the hands of a man in Richmond), and much needed a little capital to commence freedom with. A generous contribution was made by the audience.

Frederick Douglass, the eloquent and noble man, himself a slave up to the period of manhood, then took the floor, and with a few remarks introduced William and Ellen Craft, the fugitives from Georgia, to the audience.

William Craft then gave, very briefly, a sketch of their escape. After he had finished, Henry Brown, by request of many in the audience, again came forward, and sang, with much feeling and unexpected propriety, a hymn or anthem beginning, "I waited patiently for the Lord; and he inclined unto me, and heard my cry." It appeared that Brown, after first being delivered from the box in Philadelphia, and walking repeatedly up and down the room, had begged permission to sing; and thereupon burst into this anthem. If the reader will turn to the 40th Psalm, from which the words of the anthem are taken, he will see how peculiarly applicable it is to Henry Brown's situation and sufferings.

Stephen S. Foster[16] then addressed the audiences upon the guilty character and position of the American ministers and churches. He continued his remarks until the hour of adjournment arrived.

THURSDAY

Wendell Phillips then took the platform. He brought Henry (Box) Brown to his side, and eulogised his patient and disinterested heroism. Mr. Phillips offered the following resolution:

Resolved, That we sympathize deeply and warmly with those self-sacrificing and devoted heroes, who are now suffering a cruel imprisonment in the District of Columbia and the several States, for deeds of humanity and justice to their outraged and downtrodden brethren.

And further, Resolved, That the best way we know of to express efficiently our sympathy and respect, is to labor for the overthrow of that Union which builds the dungeon, and that Church which bolts its door.

彐 彑

The Liberator, June 8, 1849

Great Meeting in Faneuil Hall[17]

Speeches of Samuel J. May, Frederick
Douglass and Wendell Phillips,

Reported for the Liberator, by P. W. Leeds, Jr., Stenographer.

from SPEECH OF REV. SAMUEL J. MAY.

The recollections that crowd upon my mind as I stand on this spot, after an absence of many years—at least, they seem to me many years—and recollect the advance that has been made in the cause of the oppressed and down-trodden, are peculiarly gratifying. Well do I remember when this hall was closed against the advocates of human liberty. Well do I remember the time, in 1835, when fifteen hundred of the most influential and wealthy men in this city signed a petition for the opening of this hall to the delivery of sentiments antagonistic in their tone to the sentiments uttered by those who are only pleading that the great principles of the Declaration of our Independence might be carried out in the conduct of the nation.[18] I say, fifteen hundred gentlemen of this city petitioned for the opening of this hall, that an opposition might be manifested to the advocacy of human freedom; thereby waking up against us a spirit of violence that had well nigh bathed our native soil with our own blood.

But, Sir, these days have past [sic], and we now recall the unpleasant remembrance only to rejoice in it as evidence of the progress which has been made in the glorious cause we have espoused. Look at our country now—not by any means what she ought to be—not by any means at the high pinnacle of prosperity that our hearts, in the fondness of our confidence in the American people, foretold it would reach—still, when we contrast the present with the past, how gratifying the transition! Almost every where north of Mason and Dixon's line,[19] and in some places even south of it, those sentiments which have been execrated in times past, even in this hall, may be uttered without let or hindrance or molestation from any one. Can we not be grateful for the progress that has been made during the last twenty years, though we may naturally feel that comparatively little has been done, considering the length of time that has elapsed? But I rejoice to stand in this hall to-night. I rejoice to see such an assembly here. Notwithstanding the numerous demands that have been made on the attention of those interested in the various religious associations of our country, they have still been found disposed to come to this place in preference to any other, to listen to the sentiments that shall be uttered, and to respond, doubtless with unfeigned cordiality, to the demands that may be made on them for higher efforts and more determined and earnest exertion in carrying on to a completion the work which has been so gloriously commenced. Those of you who have attended the previous meetings of this Convention, have heard living epistles from the South, that must have spoken to your hearts as no written words could have done, calling on you, if there be a spark of humanity in your souls, to kindle it up anew until a fire still more intense than any that has yet burned within shall be in progress, and urging you on to efforts and exertions that are hourly needed to rid our country from such a curse as the institution of slavery. If you have attended the meetings of this Convention, you have seen men and women, children of God, presenting every appearance of humanity on their persons, telling the story of their escape from Southern oppression—escapes made not only at the risk of a still more cruel bondage, but at the risk of their lives. Never will the story be forgotten in our country or throughout the world, of the man—whom I trust you will all be permitted to see—who, that he might escape from Southern oppression, consented to a living entombment. He entered the box with the determination to be free or die; and as he heard the nails driven in, his fear was that death was to be his portion; yet, said he, let death come in preference to slavery! And is there one in this house who has a heart to feel, that can look on such a man as Henry Box Brown, and affirm that he may not enjoy the rights of a man in a country like ours? I happened to be in the city of Philadelphia—I have told the story to the Convention already, but I will tell it again—in the midst of the excitement that was caused by the arrival of a man in a box. I measured it myself;—*three feet one inch long, two feet long, and two feet six inches deep.* IN THAT BOX A MAN WAS ENTOMBED FOR TWENTY-SEVEN HOURS!

The box was placed in the express car in Richmond, Va., and subjected to all the rough treatment ordinarily given to boxes of merchandise; for, notwithstanding the admonition of "*this side up with care,*" the box was tumbled over, so that he was sometimes on his head; yes, at one time, for nearly two hours, as it seemed to him, on *his head*, and momentarily expecting that life would become extinct from the terrible pressure of blood that poured upon his brain. Twenty-seven hours was this man subjected to this imminent peril; but, through the blessing of God, such was the intensity of the love of life and liberty in his bosom, that it seemed to set at defiance all the principles of physiology itself, and to live without air, that he might for one moment, at least, breathe the air of liberty. (Great applause.) Does not such a man deserve to be free? Is there a heart here, that does not bid him welcome? Is there a heart here, that can doubt that there must be in him not merely the heart and soul of a deteriorated man—a degraded, inferior man—but the heart and soul of a noble man? Not a *nobleman*, sir, but a NOBLE MAN! Who can doubt it?

Sir, I confess when I see such nobleness in a man of another hue from my own, I almost wish I could change my complexion for his. (Applause and hisses.) I have been hissed before. (Great applause, and a voice said, "In good company.") Well might the arrival of such a man, in such a condition as that, excite an intense interest in the city of Philadelphia. The gentleman to whom he was consigned, spent the night previous to his arrival, sleepless. His expectation was—yes, he felt it certain—that, instead of a living man, he should find a corpse in the box coming to him. And when he found it safely deposited in his house, such was his excitement that, for a while, he dared not approach it; but having gathered about him some friends to sympathize with him in his emotion, and sustain and strengthen him to meet the worst, he approached the box, and knocking on it with his knuckles, exclaimed, "Is all right within?" and to his unspeakable joy, the response came, "ALL RIGHT!" (Great sensation.) For a while, so great was his agitation, that he could hardly use the instruments that were necessary to relieve him from his imprisonment; but when the cover was removed, a man—a true man—a noble man arose from the temporary coffin into a living life—a new life indeed, unless there be base men enough in this part of the country to allow him to be restored to the living death from which he has escaped. The moment he appeared, the gentleman to whom he had been consigned, as soon as he could give vent to his feelings, exclaimed in a burst of emotion—for he knew not what was well-nigh exactly true—"You are the greatest man in America!" (Laughter and applause.) Certainly, no man in America has done what Henry Box Brown has done. His escape will be remembered as long as the history of the struggles of Humanity for her rights shall be remembered. As soon as he was released, having walked the room, stretched his limbs, filled his lungs for the first time with the air of liberty, and gathered up into his soul a realizing sense of his deliverance, the spirit of gratitude to God came over his heart, and he burst out into an anthem that will never be forgotten, and was never sung more appropriately than then—"I waited patiently for the Lord, and he inclined unto me, and heard my cry."

from SPEECH OF WENDELL PHILLIPS

It is the slave, the fugitive slave from the plantation, whose tongue, inspired by oppression, speaks most forcibly to the American people.

I know you may charge me with exaggeration; but I want you to look at one man, at least. Here is a man, who has come into Boston, into Massachusetts, a fugitive. [Mr. Henry *Box* Brown, the escaped slave, here came upon the platform, and was received with hearty applause.] This man came from the slave plantations of the South, in the box to which my friend referred at the commencement of the meeting; and he tells us that, when the box was turned upside down, for some twenty miles, and he felt the blood rushing downward with suffocating power into his head, he resolved that he would die there, before uttering a sound that would betray him. (Cheers.)

Fellow-citizens, we stand in Faneuil Hall; and we boast that those men, whose portraits are suspended around us, were *our* fathers. But blood does not make the most real parentage. I ask you, lovers of freedom, who, in the year 1849, is the nearer child of HANCOCK[20] and ADAMS,[21] in venturing every thing for liberty, this man or ourselves? O, when history goes up and down this generation hereafter, to touch this and the other head with the torch of immortality, do you think our names will be remembered—we, who may have passed our lives reputably, decently, and at case? No; when we shall rot in the common sod, the romance, the deep and thrilling interest of the coming generation, will linger about those who, alone against a whole people, have dared every thing for liberty. These are the TELLS and the ROLANDS,[22] the true heroes of story and song. (Applause.)

You have all of you been reading Macaulay.[23] The press could not pour out its pages fast enough for you. You admired the endurance of Elizabeth Gaunt and the Duke of Argyle.[24] Elizabeth Gaunt and John, Duke of Argyle! Why, every pulpit in the country was pregnant with petitions for them. The spectators that clustered around them bade them God-speed, in spite of Jeffries and the hangman.[25] The sympathies of England sustained them in their trials. Half the land was on its knees in their behalf. Here was a man suffocating—about to die—and he knew if he died, there was hardly one press, from Maine to Georgia, but would regard his death with scorn; that there was hardly a pulpit that would put up a petition in behalf of himself or the swarming millions of his oppressed countrymen, no matter the devotion and self-sacrifice they might evince;—yet he dared to die, alone and un-pitied, for liberty. (Applause.) He took his life in his hand—looked in the faces of the white race around him, saw in none the lines of sympathy or tear of pity—and yet he shrank not. We say, in behalf of this man, whom God created, and whom law-abiding WEBSTER[26] and WINTHROP[27] swore should find no shelter on the soil of Massachusetts—we say that they may make their little motions, and pass their little laws, in Washington, but that FANEUIL HALL REPEALS THEM, in the name of the humanity of Massachusetts. (Great applause.) What shall history tell of Winthrop and Webster? Winthrop built the Custom House by his diligence in speech-making, and Webster built the mills at Lowell by his well-remunerated toil.[28] There stands the man, (pointing to Mr. GARRISON,)[29] who made us able to say, with some little share of truth,—Slaves cannot breathe in Massachusetts! They touch our country, and their shackles fall! (Applause.) WEBSTER says we are a law-abiding people. Let him come and try, in the case of these fugitives. Let him get HENRY BROWN from the fangs of the abolitionists, if he can! (Cheers.) Give us the Bible for a text-book, and Faneuil Hall for a pulpit, and we will yet control the moral sentiment of this nation, though we give you the odds of thirty thousand pro-slavery ministers. (Cheers.)

Now, friends, we draw to the close of this Convention. It falls to my lot, at this late hour, to say a few closing words to those who have come to listen to its deliberations. You may have thought that we were extravagant and unreasonable in argument; but we spoke our hearty convictions—we spoke the truth. You entered the religious anniversary meetings,[30] and you saw the platform crowded with the well-fed, the well-paid, the respectable clergy of Massachusetts. It is natural they should speak well of the institution which supports them, and which they support. This platform is crowded, but it is *with fugitive slaves*! Yes, we gather them by the dozens, to-day—fugitives from the Church and State of America. (Sensation.)

We have it stated in a Georgia paper, that Ellen Crafts [*sic*] is dead. She is dead to the slave institutions. You know when a woman enters a convent, they change her name, and cut her hair; she is considered dead to the community out of which she came, in Catholic countries. Well, Ellen Crafts has come to Massachusetts; she has changed her name; she is dead to slavery, and to the country out of which she came, and baptized, we trust, into a liberty which seeks to stay itself on the rising humanity of the Commonwealth.

I hold in my hand a paper from that savior of the slave, JONATHAN WALKER[31]—the noblest hand in all America; that on which your Government has stamped the initials, S. S.—SLAVE SAVIOR, as it should read. It contains the following resolution:

Resolved, That we sympathize deeply and warmly with those self-sacrificing and devoted heroes, who are now suffering a cruel imprisonment in the District of Columbia and the several States, for deeds of humanity and justice to their outraged and down-trodden brethren.

"Thou shalt love thy neighbor as thyself," says the Great Master. Here are two men who have most pre-eminently obeyed the command from the Mount. Do you hear any such expressions of sympathy in any religious gathering in Boston? I trow[32] not. I have added, on the other side of this resolution, the following:

And further, Resolved, That the best way we know of to express efficiently our sympathy and respect, is to labor for the overthrow of that Union which builds the dungeon, and that Church which bolts its door.

Now, friends, and Mr. Chairman, we do not make this nation. We are a small band of individuals, with but little influence, and with but few years over our heads to give us time for influence. This nation and its institutions have come out of the bosom of American Christianity and American law. All the faults we find with them are traceable to these.

Fellow-citizens, when such a man as FREDERICK DOUGLASS tells you his history, the result of American prejudice—speaks the honest indignation of his race against his wrongs—when he tells you of your own conduct towards him—keep your hands by your sides. Hush those echoing plaudits of yours; keep silent. What right have you to applaud? What have you done to aid the slave to his liberty? What have you done to open this Hall for his welcome? None but clean hands have the right to welcome this hero of the box; those only that have labored to create that public sentiment here which alone encouraged him to his hardy attempt. You who swear so often personally, or by deputy, to support the laws from which he fled, why do you bless his flight? Can he find shelter in any pulpit in Boston? How many? One, two, or three, alone. Do one of two things—confess that your hearts blush for the deeds your hands are not ashamed to do; or go, coin your plaudits into statutes, and then we will all cry, "God save the slave sheltering Commonwealth of Massachusetts!"

─❧❧─

The Farmer's Cabinet, June 14, 1849

(From the *Boston Republican*.)

Henry Box Brown.

Appendix B : 137

[printed also, with a different introduction, under the title "Thrilling Narrative" in the *Friends' Weekly Intelligencer*, June 30, 1849]

One of the most thrilling events of the week was the appearance of the heroic man who so recently escaped from slavery in a box, marked and forwarded as Merchandise, from Richmond to Philadelphia. The warmest sympathies of the people were enlisted in his behalf. His story is one of thrilling interest. Every generous heart will be touched by its recital; whenever and wherever that story is told it will arouse the sympathies of mankind, not only for Henry Box Brown, but for his oppressed race. Shame on Virginia, that one of her sons should thus be compelled to act and suffer to gain the rights which belong to our common humanity. She proudly claims to be mother of statesmen and heroes, but no son of hers ever gave greater evidence of heroism than this poor despised son of hers. And this act of heroism was not made in her defense, but it was made in escaping from her bosom.

We copy from the Chronotype[33] the story as told by himself, at the anti-slavery meeting on Wednesday night. Let each of us, as we read it, remember that three millions of our race are held in bondage, by the same laws which this poor man risked so much to escape from. Let each one of us, then, firmly resolve to exert all the political and moral influence we possess to free the country from the curse and shame of slavery. Let us vow, that come what may, we will never cease our efforts until every slave in our country can stand up in the dignity of manhood and say, "I too am a man and a brother."

THRILLING NARRATIVE—At the meeting on Wednesday evening, a fugitive slave, newly named Henry *Box* Brown, came on to the platform, by invitation and related his adventures, while escaping from the house of bondage.

Henry was a slave in Virginia. He has, or had, a wife and three children, for whom their master asked $650. The husband and father made incredible exertions to purchase them, and succeeded in raising $600. The remaining $50 were advanced by his own master, who had a lien upon the wife and children. After buying his family, Henry rented a house for them, but he soon became involved as his master claimed the largest portion of his earnings. One morning he went off to his work, but on returning found that his wife and children had been seized, sold upon the auction block to the slave traders, and were to be transported out of the State. They were sold for $1,050. After this sad event, his master seized upon the furniture provided for the slave wife, sold it and pocketed the proceeds.

Henry remarked, with the deepest pathos, that after his wife and children were stolen, his heart was broken. He had learned to sing to lighten the tedium of his labor, and for the gratification of his fellow-captives, but now he could not sing. His thoughts were far away in the rice swamps of Carolina or the cotton plantations of Georgia. His wife was not and his children were not, and he refused to be comforted. When his master, noticing his despondency, told him he could get another wife—southern morality—Brown shook his head,—the wife of his affections and the children of his love, or none at all.

Thoughts of liberty now began to spring up in his bosom. He had heard of the abolitionists, and determined to escape to them if it was possible. He became frugal, saved with more than a miser's eagerness every cent he could lay claim to, until he had amassed a sufficient sum for his purpose. The means used for escape were of the most unprecedented character. With the assistance of a friend, arrangements were made for him to escape in a box, which was to be forwarded to friends of the slave in Philadelphia, carefully marked as a valuable package.

The *friend* who assisted in this plot, took all his money, about $80, and his clothes. Brown could offer no objections, though it left him penniless. Yet with a Roman heart, he was true to the fixed purpose of his soul; he was on his way to liberty. The box used for this extraordinary flight was only *three feet one inch long, two feet wide, and two feet six inches deep*. In this diminutive box he was transported from Richmond to Philadelphia by railroad and steamboat, a distance of three hundred miles, amid perils so great that the mind shudders when they are contemplated.

On board of the steamboat while going up the Potomac, the box was set on end, which placed Brown *head downward*. How long he remained in this fearful position, he does not know, but he mentally resolved to die, if die he must without making a sign, which might involve those who had been assisting him.

The next great peril which he encountered was at the Baltimore depot at Washington. The box was roughly tumbled out of the transportation wagon, and it rolled over two or three times. This the unhappy fugitive thought was bad enough, but he was horror stricken when it was proposed not to forward the box until the next day. In that event he would die. But he bethought him to pray, and while yet praying a superior officer ordered it to be forwarded. When put into the baggage car he was again placed on his head, in which position he remained for the space of half an hour. His eyes became swollen nearly out of his head; his veins were filled to bursting, and he must have died, had not the position been providentially changed.

The box arrived safely in Philadelphia to its destination. The friends who were anxiously waiting for it were assembled in a room with the door locked. They were afraid to move. They feared that the inmate was dead, as he made no noise. Finally one, more firm than the rest, rapped on the box, "Is all right here?" in a friendly tone. "All right," was the brief response from within. The friends were overcome by their emotions, and one of them, finding speech exclaimed, "You are the greatest man in America."

As for Brown he was joyful, his fatigues were nothing, his sufferings were forgotten. He was free; he breathed the air of liberty. That one thought swallowed up all others. After stretching himself for a moment, he breathed forth the feelings of his soul in a song of solemn praise for his deliverance. Without premeditation he burst out in a singularly melodious voice this appropriate anthem:

"I waited patiently, and the Lord my God delivered me."

What heroism, what self denial, what energy of purpose are here manifested. The sincerity and strength of faith in the Providence of God we must admire and respect. Such a man has been added to the freemen of the North. Let him be received as a brother beloved.—When our columns are less crowded we shall give the interesting narrative of Ellen and William Craft, fugitive slaves from Georgia.

-ⴺ ⴾ-

Christian Inquirer, June 16, 1849

The Anti-Slavery Convention

Was, of course, as usual, a point of attraction; and characterized, as usual, by the power, freshness, truth, eccentricity, extravagance and boundless freedom, of its discussions. Women spoke. Some of the orators denounced, in sweeping terms, the American church and clergy; and yet, Rev. Messrs. Sumner, Lincoln, J. Russell, Dale, S. J. May, and other Ministers of different denominations, appeared on the platform as advocates of Abolitionism, and were among its most earnest friends. Probably the distinction made by Rev. S. J. May, between "Priestianity" and "Christianity," explains the apparent inconsistency. The Free Soil party[34] was handled without gloves. FOSTER dealt out his bold denunciations; GARRISON exhibited his courageous and uncompromising spirit; WENDELL PHILLIPS, with graceful and yet scorching eloquence, and keen, close argument, ably maintained his well-known extreme position and radical opinions; whilst FREDERICK DOUGLASS—whether dealing in humourous stories, exposing, in his view, the sophistry and inhumanity of the Colonization Society, or combating the prejudice against color, or withstanding the storm of opposition his mere words had raised—appeared as the natural and most accomplished orator, holding in his power, and moving at his will, an audience, many of whom were far from friendly; and proving that he, at least stood up an entire confutation of the asserted natural inferiority of his race. The meetings were, of course, at times, disturbed and disorderly; but less so, we believe, than heretofore. The ultra-Abolitionists certainly show great tact and indomitable zeal; and they understand stage-effect. This year they produced a "sensation," by exhibiting fugitive slaves; and, omitting other matters we meant to put on record, we close this summary, without comment, with an account of one case of heroism shown in the pursuit of freedom, certainly without parallel in history. Our reference is to Henry—hereafter, doubtless, to be known, and sent down to posterity as

Henry Box Brown.

This man was actually transported a distance of *three hundred miles*, through a slave-holding territory, and by public thoroughfares, in a box the dimensions of which, as taken by Rev. S. J. May, are exactly as follows: *three feet one inch long; two feet wide and two feet six inches deep.*

While at Richmond, though the box was legibly and distinctly marked, "this side up with care," it was placed on end with his head downwards. He felt strange pains, and was preparing himself to die, preferring liberty or death to slavery, and he gave no sign. He was however relieved from this painful position, and encountered no other danger than the rough handling of the box, until it arrived at Washington. When the porters who had charge of it reached the depot there, they threw or dropped it with violence to the ground, and it rolled down a small hill, turning over two or three times. This he thought was bad enough, but the words he heard, filled him with anguish, and brought with them the blackness of despair. They were, that the box was so heavy it could not be forwarded that night, but must lay over twenty-four hours. In the language of the fugitive, "My heart swelled in my throat; I could scarcely breathe; great sweats came over me; I gave up all hope.—But it was put into my remembrance that the preacher had said[,] It is good to pray at all times. So I tried to pray. "Lord Jesus, put it into the hearts of these men to find a way to send this box forward." While I was yet praying, a man came in and said, "That box must go on; it's the express mail." Oh, what relief I felt. It was taken into the depot, and I was placed head downwards again for the space of half an hour. My eyes were swollen almost out of my head, and I was fast becoming insensible, when the position was changed."

He arrived in Philadelphia after many hair-breadth 'scapes, and the box was taken to the house to which it was directed. The panting inmate heard voices whispering; afterwards more men came in. They were doubtful or fearful about opening the box. He lay still, not knowing who the people were. Finally, one of them knocked on the box, and asked, "Is all right here?" "All right," echoed from the box. The finale of this simple tale was received with deafening shouts.

In corroboration of it, Rev. S. J. May said he was in Philadelphia in the midst of the excitement caused by this wonderful adventure. He said that, for obvious reasons, he could not give the name of the gentleman to whom the box was consigned, but he knew him as a warm-hearted friend of humanity. That gentleman had told him, Mr. M., that when the box arrived at his house, he was overcome with agitation. The man might be dead. He hoped, yet feared. It might be necessary to call a coroner. He finally assembled several true friends, and then tremblingly asked, "Is all right here?" The voice came up as from the grave, "All right." The reaction of his feelings was so great as to stop his breath; but when he could speak, he wildly exclaimed, "You are the greatest man in America."

The fugitive when released, after stretching his limbs, did not appear fatigued. The glorious sense of freedom was upon him in his heart, pervading his whole being, and burst out into song. This was the appropriate anthem of deliverance:
"I waited patiently, and the Lord hath delivered me."

⊰ ⊱

The North Star, August 10, 1849

From the *Dover (N.H.) Morning Star*

THE FUGITIVE'S WIFE

BY J. W. BARKER

His thoughts were far away amid the rice swamps of Carolina, or the cotton plantations of Georgia; his wife was not, his children were not, and he would not be comforted. — Narrative of Henry Box Brown

O where have ye borne them, the friends of my heart?
They are gone from my cabin away!
Have they fallen a prey to the slaveholder's mart,
While I have been toiling today?

I miss the kind hand and the care-soothing voice,
That were all upon earth I could claim;
I call for the heart that alone can rejoice
At my pleasure, or lighten my pain.

It echoes not back at the sound of mine own,
No footsteps are lightsome and free;
O where have ye borne them away from my home,
My friends that were all unto me?

Methinks I can hear, far away in the South,
Mid the rice swamps, a voice of despair;
Upon every breeze it is murmuring forth,
That my wife and my children are there.

I can hear it resound mid the rustle of canes,
In the fields of that whitening soil;
The crack of the slavedriver's merciless whip,
That is urging them forward to toil.

And the tear that is scalding that fair sable cheek,
As she bends by the dark orange tree,
Hath volumes of tenderness tongue cannot speak,
That her heart is still lingering with me.

She was mine, till the beck of the slavedriver's power
Hath summoned her quickly away,
To toil mid the cotton-fields far in the South,
'Neath the sun of a long weary day.

O talk not of others that can comfort my heart,
And banish this night of despair, —
The friend of my bosom, the friend of my youth,
Is toiling in loneliness there.

Come back to my bosom, it beateth for thee,
In dreams of our long-vanished bliss;
Come back—but the fetter on "spirit and heal"
Denieth us pleasure like this.

Great God, in that land where the spirit resides,
That they tell us is glorious and fair,
Will the slavedriver's whip be heard on that shore?
Are there shackles and auction-blocks there?

·≒ ⊨·

The Liberator, September 14, 1849

Henry Box Brown.

Mr. Brown has had his Narrative written from a statement of facts
made by himself, accompanied with remarks upon the remedy
for slavery, by Charles Stearns. It makes a pamphlet of ninety
pages, and is accompanied by a pretty good likeness of the hero
of the box, whose marvellous escape from slavery is so well known
and authenticated. It is to be regretted that it was not prepared
with more care, as its loose and declamatory style greatly mars
its interest; still, there is much in it calculated to affect the heart,
and to excite an intense moral abhorrence of the cruel system of
slavery.

·≒ ⊨·

Christian Register, September 22, 1849

Recent Pamphlets

HENRY BOX BROWN. This narrative is written by Mr. Charles
Stearns from statements made by Mr. Brown. We wish the com-
piler had not worked the matter up quite as much, and had given
it in a style of greater verisimilitude, more simplicity and better
taste, and mixed it less up with irrelevant matter. "A round, unvarnished tale"[35] of this refuge from slavery, would be one of the
strongest weapons for anti-slavery ever employed. The engraved

likeness is not a good nor a true one. The print of the box, on the outside cover, with its label, has affected us more than any representation ever made to us, and we say, — God speed the day when the aspirations for liberty that encountered the terrible hazard to life of such a way of escape, may be universally fulfilled in the redemption of every bondman and bondwoman in the land.

⊰ ⊱

The North Star, September 28, 1849

NARRATIVE OF HENRY BOX BROWN, who escaped from Slavery in a box three feet long, two wide, and two and a half high. Bela Marsh, Cornhill, Boston. Price 25 cents.

What will not a man do for freedom? Slaveholders tell us that slaves are contented and happy. Behold the proof! To escape from that state of happiness which, according to the Southern doctrine, is the perfect and natural condition of the negro, we find him enduring all sorts of strange and unheard-of hardships. At one time, he is seen, cold worn out, and perishing, hiding from the bloodhound — biped and quadruped, in marshes and forests; at another time, secreting himself in the hold of a steam-boat in imminent risk of suffocation; at another, as in this case of the adventurous Henry Box Brown, cramped up and packed away, like so much merchandise, in a box three feet by two. America has the melancholy honor of being the sole producer of such books as this. She is so busy talking about the doctrine of human rights, that she has not time to put it in practice. Boasting forever of her republican institutions, where shall we find the nation that has less reason to boast? Shouting continually about freedom, and human equality; but in practice denying the existence of either. The narrator, commencing his story of wrong, says that he is not about to horrow the feelings of the reader by a terrific representation of the untold horrors of Slavery. He will present the beautiful side of the picture and will relate stories of partial kindness on the part of his master, and of comparative enjoyment on his own part. He never, during his thirty years of bondage, received a whipping. It was not

146 : Appendix B

for fear of bodily torture, that he suffered himself to be coffined alive. Is there nothing besides this, in slavery, to be feared?

Henry Box Brown was born a slave in Louisa county, Va., forty-five miles from the city of Richmond. His mother was a religious woman, and used to instruct him in the principles of morality. She taught him not to steal and not to lie. From some other quarter, his youthful mind got hold of the idea that his master was Almighty God, and his young master Jesus Christ. While a young lad, his chief employment was waiting upon his master and mistress with, at intervals, lessons in the cultivation of the plantation, with the fearful apprehension hanging upon his mind, that the time was not far distant when he should be driven to daily toil beneath the rays of the scorching sun. He was anxious to learn the condition of the slaves on other plantations, and did not lose any opportunity of gratifying his curiosity. He and his brother were in the practice of carrying grain to a mill twenty miles distant. On one occasion, while waiting for their grain, they saw a number of forlorn-looking beings pass, who, as they passed looked with astonishment at the two colored persons with shoes, vests, and hats on. The brothers followed these poor creatures to their quarters, and entered into conversation with them, which was soon cut short by the approach of the overseer. They had not gone far when they heard their screams while suffering under the lash for the crime of talking to strangers. Henry and his brother felt thankful that they were exempted from such terrible treatment, but were filled with apprehension. By and bye their master died. As he was about to expire, he sent for the two brothers. They ran to his bedside with beating hearts, expecting to be set free. The unrepentant slaveholder's dying bequest was, "I have given you to my son William, and you must obey him." After this, he was taken to Richmond, to work in his young master's tobacco manufactory. The overseer of this establishment was a bad man. He used to rob and cheat his employer, who never suspected anything of the kind. He thought Mr. Allen was always right. This man was a church member, and was very devout and regular in his attendance on public worship. He prayed long and loudly with the pupils in the Sabbath school; but was often heard to say that he thought it all "a d—— lie" that niggers could be converted; for they had no souls. Another part of his creed was that a white man might do as he liked, provided he read the Bible and joined the church. As Henry grew up, he began to think about finding a wife; and formed an acquaintance with a young woman named Nancy. He learned to love Nancy. Her master was a pious man, and promised Henry Brown, if he married her, that she should never be sold. After their masters had talked the matter over, and given their permission, they were married. About a year after, the pious Mr. Lee forgot his promise, and sold Henry's wife. She now became the property of a saddler, one of Dr. Plummer's church members. This man's wife used her cruelly. Not long after she was again sold to a Mr. Cartrell, another member of Dr. Plummer's church. This man induced Henry Brown to pay him $50.00, to assist him in the purchase; and also $50.00 a-year for her time; and for a season all went smoothly. But soon came the crowning catastrophe. It was on a pleasant morning in August 1846 (says, Henry Brown,) I left my wife and three little children safely in our little home, and proceeded to my labor. I felt that although I was a slave, there were many alleviations to my cup of sorrow. I felt that life was not all a blank to me—that there were some pure joys yet my portion. That day, as he continues his sad story, as the hour approached when he should take his little prattling children on his knee, he was told that his wife and smiling babes were locked in prison, and that to-morrow's sun would see them on their way to the distant South. He attempted to persuade his master to buy his wife; but he would not; he tried to persuade others to do it, but all in vain. The next day (he proceeds) I stationed myself by the road, along which the slaves were to pass. The purchaser of my wife was a Methodist minister, who was about starting for North Carolina. Pretty soon five waggon-loads of little children passed and looking at the foremost, I saw a little child pointing its tiny hand towards me, and saying "There's my father!" It was my eldest child. Soon the gang approached in which his wife was chained. He seized her hand, intending to bid her farewell; but words failed him. He accompanied her for some distance, with her hand clasped in his, but could not speak, and was compelled to turn silently away.

Henry Brown then relates the particulars of his journey from slavery to freedom. The story is soon told. After this cruel separation, he could think of nothing, but how to escape from slavery. He prayed earnestly to Heaven for guidance. The thought darted into his mind "get a box, and put yourself in it." He got the box and carried it to his friend who had promised to assist him, who inquired, when he saw it, if it was to put his clothes in. No, said he, it is to put Henry Brown in. Henry's friend was astonished, as well he might be; but upon his insisting, he finally consented. The box was taken to the Express office, and although directed "This side up with care," it was placed on its end; so that the candidate for liberty started with his head downwards. From thence it was carried to the depot, and tumbled roughly into the baggage wagon—"right side up" this time. He was then put on board a steamboat, head downwards again, and so remained for an hour and a half; but as he had resolved on "victory or death," he endured the pain of his eyes bursting from their sockets, with the courage of a martyr. Soon a cold sweat covered him from head to foot. He expected that every minute would be his last. He prayed to God for deliverance. He overheard one of the passengers say to another, "We have been here two hours, and have travelled twenty miles, let us sit down and rest ourselves." They turned over his box, and sat upon it. They wondered what the box contained. One of them guessed it was the mail. On arriving at Washington, he again fell on his head. He was then rolled down a declivity, when he thought his neck was dislocated by the violence of the concussion; and then to add to his misery, he heard some one say, "there is no room for this box; it will have to remain behind," but in a short time, directions were given to place it aboard. The box was then tumbled into the car—head downwards again. More baggage was taken in at a stopping place not far on the road; and the good Samaritan of a baggage-master placed him "right side up." The box reached Philadelphia at three o'clock in the morning. At six o'clock a wagon drove up, and a voice was heard inquiring for a box. It was the box he wanted. They were not long in getting it carried to the house, where a number of persons were waiting to receive it. Now is an anxious moment. They crowd around, doubting whether the box contains a dead body or a living man. At last one ventures to rap upon the box, and with a trembling voice asks—"Is all right within?" To which the one time slave, but now freeman, replies "All right!" Then the box is opened, and Henry Box Brown appears, a noble specimen of humanity, who has dared and suffered for freedom in such a way as was never before dreamed of.

Such is a very imperfect sketch of this interesting Narrative. We say to all our readers, Get the book.

⌐◨ ◧¬

New York Evangelist, October 4, 1849

Henry Box Brown

The Chronotype narrates the thrilling adventures of the life of this fugitive slave, as follows:

Brown is an earnest religious man, bearing the index of stability and fidelity in his countenance. In spite of slavery, the ideas of Christian purity and benevolence had taken hold of him. He fastened his heart to a wife, and the attachment had been cemented by three promising children. But one day the auctioneer's hammer came down upon all four, and they were *gone*. "Never fret about it," said his master, "Marry another wife and get some more children." The iron of that speech entered his soul. He began, with every fibre of the manhood in him, to plot his escape. No fool of a task is that, where every eye of every white man has nothing to do but to watch you, and every dog and every newspaper will bark on your track, and where, if you fail, tortures like the Inquisition's await you.

Henry had got possession of $166, and no financier in State street could have husbanded it better, though the first investment did not turn out so good as it might have been. He bought *a friend* with half of it. With him he consulted about the means of escape, anxiously, but to no purpose. At last, in answer to earnest prayer, as Henry says, it occurred to him to box himself up. He did it, enclosing with himself only a bladder of water, as a *medicine* for the journey.

The box was properly addressed to a friend in Philadelphia, marked with the always ludicrously unheeded words, "this side up with care."—The "friend" was put under a solemn pledge to accompany the box to its destination, and *see* to it. But he took it in his *friendly* head, as a purchased friend naturally would, merely to tumble the box into the express office at Richmond and *telegraph* the consignee in Philadelphia of the fact. There was obviously no remedy for Brown. He seems to have been destined to undergo the fate of mere merchandise, for "an ensample" [*sic*] to the American people. As such he was put through in the modern fashion, *with* dispatch and *without* care. After waiting some time *on his head* at the express office, he was carted to the *depot*, and happened to fall *right side up* in the freight car. But on the Potomac steamer he rode nearly two hours on his head, till his eyes protruded and he was on the point of suffocation, when he prayed earnestly, and, as it is in older cases on record, the Lord heard him and sent two passengers, one of whom said, "Well we have come twenty miles in two hours, now let's sit down and rest ourselves," and the two turned over his box and sat on it.

These angels of God's mercy speculated on the contents of the box, as they sat on it, and concluded it must contain the *mail*. At Washington he fell again on his head, and came near being left, but prayer again brought an angel in the shape of a gentleman, who said, "That box came with the mail, and it must go on with it." In it was thrown, Brown's head downwards again, a mistake, however, which was rectified on righting the baggage at the next stopping place.

Twenty-seven hours from Richmond brought the box to the depot in the Quaker city, where it waited from 3 A.M. to 6 A.M. when the consignee, or receiving angel, with a mild voice and straight coat of course, called and wished to know if a box, marked so and so, was there. "Yes." The freight was settled, and the box trucked to a wagon, and soon set down in the friend's parlor, where a circle of friends were waiting to witness—a resurrection. What a moment! There is the silent box. Is there a listening, knowing, strong-souled man in it, or a carcass fit for the dissecting room? To Brown, too, it was a crisis. Was he among friends? Was he north of the slavery line? Had his perils been for nothing, or was he at last to draw free breath through more than three gimblet [sic] holes? He had the advantage of the outsiders. The voices of those Quaker women could have left no doubt in his mind that the hour of his delivery was approaching. There the box stood, and no Quaker meal ever had the blessing of so silent a Quaker grace. At last some good soul mustered the courage, with throbbing heart, to rap on the lid and ask, "Is all right?" "All right!" from within. "Here—hammers, axes, chisels, pincers—tear off the cover." Tears streamed with the work. The tough nails gave way on all sides, the pine cracked, the grave opened, and up rose the *live* man, but sunk back again in a swoon.—"Air, water, let him breathe"—he was alive again. Up rose a humble, but strong prophet, whose voice is now touching thousands of breasts as with live coals from God's altar—to kindle them against slavery.

⊰ ⊱

The Rural Repository Devoted to Polite Literature, Such as Moral and Sentimental Tales, Original Communications, Biography, Traveling Sketches, Poetry, Amusing Miscellany, Humorous and Historical Anecdotes, October 1849

LITERARY WORLD.

Narrative of Henry Box Brown, who escaped from slavery, enclosed in a box three feet long, two wide, and two and a half high. Written from a statement of facts made by himself. With remarks upon the remedy for slavery. By Charles Stearns, Boston: Brown & Stearns. For sale by Bela Marsh, 25 Cornhill.

Here is another thrilling narrative of an escape from slavery. In reading this volume, and the stirring descriptions of Watson,

Clarke, Brown, Douglass and Henson,[36] we find indeed a new department of literature; a department, however, not very creditable to America, but which no other country could furnish. This stock of literature is rapidly filing up. Every fresh escape from the land of darkness furnishes materials for a new volume. And we apprehend these escapes will be much more frequent, though we seriously doubt whether there will be any narratives more exciting than those already furnished. Though we have no apology for slavery, yet it is remarkable to see how genius contrives to burst its fetters. Like the prison, it sometimes concentrates the whole genius. And the reader who wants to peruse one of the most thrilling exhibitions of genius, under the most discouraging circumstances, would do well to purchase the narrative before us.

-ᏋᏋ-

The North Star, November 16, 1849, reprinted from the *Practical Christian*

Henry Box Brown in Milford.

It was a few minutes past the hour at which the meeting was appointed when he arrived, and the Hall was then crowded. But the people had not done coming; they came long afterwards and brought in seats, and finally stood up in the vacant places about the aisles. The earnest attention of this large company bore ample testimony to the thrilling interest which his sufferings and escape created in their minds. Their hearts and their pockets answered the call made upon them, and the general cause of Anti-Slavery as well as his individual case received an impulse by it. When the incidents of a life in, and an escape from slavery are crowded into an hour's time, there must be some rather sudden passages from the pathetic to the ludicrous. There are several such passages in his narrative, and the audience answered accordingly; and at the close of his song the singer was greeted with a hearty round of clapping. These demonstrations on the part of the audience were a little annoying to some of the Methodist friends. There had been a funeral at the Church during the day, which of course rendered their minds more liable to be grieved by such matters than they otherwise would have been.

His narrative is certainly a swift witness against what passes for Christianity in the land. Every person concerned in the cruelties which he suffered was a professed Christian. The claimer of himself, (who, when he besought him to purchase his wife and children, to save them from separation, bid him get another wife,) was a Presbyterian; the claimer and seller of his wife and children was an Episcopalian; and their purchaser a Methodist minister!

⧎ ⧎

From *Cousin Ann's Stories for Children* (Philadelphia: J. M. McKim, 1849). The story of Henry Box Brown appears on pages 22-26 of the 36-page book of stories and poems.

[the book's preface]

To My Little Readers

Dear Children:

I will tell you how I came to think of making this little book: I love children, and it would be pleasant to me to see you, and talk with you about many things. It is not very long since I was a little child myself, and played "Blind man's buff," and "Frog in the Sea," as merrily as any of you. But there are many thousands of you; and I cannot see all your faces, and talk with every one of you: so I thought I would write a little book, and that would be a good way to speak with you, though I am far away. I hope you will like it. I shall be pleased if you learn something good and pleasant from it. You will soon be men and women, and I want you to grow wiser and better every day. Then you will be happy, and God will bless you and keep you.

"Cousin Ann."[37]

Henry Box Brown

I will tell you the story of Henry Box Brown. It is a strange tale, and it is all true. Henry was a slave in Richmond, Virginia, and then

HENRY BOX BROWN.

Henry Brown Arrives. Engraving from *Cousin Ann's Stories for Children*. Philadelphia: Merrihew & Thompson, 1849. Courtesy of The Historical Society of Pennsylvania.

his name was Henry Brown. He had a wife and four little children whom he loved very much.

One night when he went home to his little hut, his children and their mother, were gone, and poor Henry found they had been sold to a trader, and were taken away to Carolina. It made him almost crazy to hear this dreadful news. He felt sure he should never see them again, for he was a slave, and would not be allowed to go after them. He had to work away for his master, just as if nothing had happened. But he thought every day about his family, and he was very sad. He thought what hard times they would have when the overseer, with his whip, drove them to work in the cotton field. He feared they would have none to be kind to them, and love them; for the traders often sell the mother to one master, and the little children to others, and they never meet again. At last, Henry thought he would try to get to a free state. He resolved that, live or die, he would not be a slave much longer. So he set to thinking how he should get off. He was afraid to run away, lest he should be caught and sent back. A slave is not allowed to travel without his master's leave. But he hit upon a lucky thought. He got a box just large enough to hold him when he was sitting down, with his head a little bent. The box was three feet long, two feet eight inches deep, and twenty-three and a half inches wide. Then, he got a kind man to send word to a trusty friend in Philadelphia, that the box would be sent on the cars to Philadelphia, on a certain day. On the top of the box was written in large black letters, "this side up with care." When it was nearly time for the cars to start, Henry took a bladder of water, some biscuit, and a large gimlet, and got into his box. Then a man nailed down the top, and porters took the box to the cars, thinking, I suppose, that it was a box of goods. It was very hot in the box, and Henry could hardly breathe, there was so little air. But he had made up his mind to die rather than make a noise, for then he would be found out, and sent back into slavery. Part of the way, he travelled by water, and when the box was put on the steamboat, it was placed so that Henry's head and back were down; but he heard people moving about, and he feared they would hear him if he turned; so he kept quite still.

He lay in this way, while the boat went twenty miles, and it nearly killed him; he said the veins in his temples were great ridges that felt as big as his finger. While Henry was lying with his head down, some men came and sat on the box, and he thought he heard one of them wonder what was in it. He staid in his little box-house twenty-six hours; but he could not eat any of his biscuit, and instead of drinking the water, he used it to bathe his hot face. Most likely, he would have died if he had not bathed his face with the water. There he sat in the dark, sometimes fanning himself with his hat; and four times he bored a hole with the gimlet, to let in a little fresh air. At last, on nearly the last day of March, 1849, the cars stopped in Philadelphia, and soon Henry felt the porters carrying him to the house of the kind man who was to receive him. The man shut the street door when the porters were gone, but he was afraid Henry was smothered, so he tapped with his fingers on the top of the box and asked, "all right?" "All right, sir," said a voice in the box. Quickly the top of the box was knocked off, and Henry stood up. He shook hands with his new friend, and he was so happy that he hardly knew what to do. After he had bathed himself and ate breakfast, he sang a hymn of praise, which he had kept in his mind to sing if he should ever get to a land of freedom in safety. The first lines were,

"I waited patiently for the Lord
And He inclined and heard me."

Henry was a strong, fine looking man. He was named Henry Box Brown, because he came nearly three hundred miles in a box. We call people heroes who do something that is brave and great, and Henry is a hero. Every body but the slaveholders seems glad of his escape from slavery. Henry will be well off in the free states, but his heart will always ache when he thinks of his wife and dear children. No one in Carolina is allowed to teach a slave to read or write; so he will never get a letter from any of his family, and it is not likely they will hear from him, or ever know that he is free.

⚑

The Liberator, September 6, 1850

Attempt to Kidnap Henry Box Brown

An attack was made on Henry Box Brown, the fugitive slave, in Providence, on Friday, by some men whose purposes were not fully disclosed. We are told that Mr. Brown was twice attacked, while walking peaceably through the streets, and at one time the attempt was made to force him into a carriage. He proved too strong for them. His friends think the object was to get him on board a vessel bound to Charleston, or to dispose of him Southward, in some other way.

The following is the Police record in the Providence Post, relative to the affair:—

Thomas Kelton was fined $15 and costs for an assault on Henry Box Brown. Appealed.

It appeared, in evidence, that Henry was passing quietly up Broad street on Friday afternoon, when he was attacked by Kelton and others, and severely beaten without any known cause. It was admitted, however, that Kelton was intoxicated. If we are not mistaken, the fine and costs were paid, when an idea struck the counsel for the defendant, and an appeal was taken. It was probably understood that Mr. Brown's business would not admit of his remaining in the city until the next session of the Court of Common Pleas.

⚑

Frederick Douglass' Paper, August 27, 1852

New York, Aug. 17th, 1852

Frederick Douglass: My Dear Friend:—Although unknown to you, I call you by that appellation, and so I would every individual who has done, and still continues to do so much for the telling millions who are held in the most horrible slavery, the sun ever shone on. In a worthless pro-slavery paper of this city, I read yesterday an account of the evil workings of some cotton-ocracy or slavedriver of the South, using his influence in England (at a place called Wolverhampton) to write down the panorama now being exhibited here by Henry Box Brown, representing it to be an exaggeration of the evil of slavery. But I was happy to find that a jury of my native country did not think so, and awarded Brown a verdict of $500 against the libeller.[38] My dear sir, I know what slavery is in all its horrors. No one better; and I can only say that no artist can exaggerate slavery wither [*sic*] in act, or deed; and it requires an "imprinted" language such as does not exist on our earth to pourtray [*sic*] the enormities and horrible cruelties practiced on the poor suffering black at this day. In the chivalrous State of South Carolina they use the most ingenious mode of torture to their domestics, or house servants, that the mind of man can devise. Such as catting, making them stand on hot ashes, heating iron to a white heat, and piercing the epidemics [*sic*]. Perhaps you may wish to know what catting means. It is this: Baring the body to the hips, and making the poor sufferer lay in a horizontal position, and then getting a large cat—a live cat, my dear sir, and applying him or her to the most tender parts thereby, pulling or pinching the tail violently. The cat tries to retain its hold, and buries its claws in the flesh, causing the blood to flow at every operation. I tell you, my dear sir, over and over again, that slavery in its horrible deformity cannot be exaggerated; and if it cannot be abolished peaceably, it ought to be forcibly. It appears all arguments, all persuasions and threats are of no avail. I, for one, am willing to sacrifice the last drop of blood I have in my veins, when the time comes for our poor degraded brethren.

Yours, Jonas Pekel

From Still, *Underground Rail Road*, 81–86[39]

Henry Box Brown

Arrived by Adams' Express

Although the name of HENRY BOX BROWN has been echoed over the land for a number of years, and the simple facts connected with his marvelous escape from slavery in a box published widely through the medium of Anti-slavery papers, nevertheless it is not unreasonable to suppose that very little is generally known in relation to this case.

Briefly, the facts are these, which doubtless have never before been fully published —

Brown was a man of invention as well as a hero. In point of interest, however, his case is no more remarkable than many others. Indeed, neither before nor after escaping did he suffer one-half what many others have experienced.

He was decidedly an unhappy piece of property in the city of Richmond, Va. In the condition of a slave he felt that it would be impossible for him to remain. Full well did he know, however, that it was no holiday task to escape the vigilance of Virginia slave-hunters, or the wrath of an enraged master for committing the unpardonable sin of attempting to escape to a land of liberty. So Brown counted well the cost before venturing upon this hazardous undertaking. Ordinary modes of travel he concluded might prove disastrous to his hopes; he, therefore, hit upon a new invention altogether, which was to have himself boxed up and forwarded to Philadelphia direct by express. The size of the box and how it was to be made to fit him most comfortably, was of his own ordering. Two feet eight inches deep, two feet wide, and three feet long were the exact dimensions of the box, lined with baize. His resources with regard to food and water consisted of the following: One bladder of water and a few small biscuits. His mechanical implement to meet the death-struggle for fresh air, all told, was one large gimlet. Satisfied that it would be far better to peril his life for freedom in this way than to remain under the galling yoke of Slavery, he entered his box, which was safely nailed up and hooped with five hickory hoops, and was then addressed by his next friend, James A. Smith, a shoe dealer, to Wm. H. Johnson, Arch street, Philadelphia, marked, "This side up with care." In this condition he was sent to Adams' Express office in a dray, and thence by overland express to Philadelphia. It was twenty-six hours from the time he left Richmond until his arrival in the City of Brotherly Love. The notice, "This side up, &c.," did not avail with the different expressmen, who hesitated not to handle the box in the usual rough manner common to this class of men. For a while they actually had the box upside down, and had him on his head for miles. A few days before he was expected, certain intimation was conveyed to a member of the Vigilance Committee that a box might be expected by the three o'clock morning train from the South, which might contain a man. One of the most serious walks he ever took—and they had not been a few—to meet and accompany passengers, he took at half past two o'clock that morning to the depot. Not once, but for more than a score of times, he fancied the slave would be dead. He anxiously looked while the freight was being unloaded from the cars, to see if he could recognize a box that might contain a man; one alone had that appearance, and he confessed it really seemed as if there was the scent of death about it. But on inquiry, he soon learned that it was not the one he was looking after, and he was free to say he experienced a marked sense of relief. That same afternoon, however, he received from Richmond a telegram, which read thus, "Your case of goods is shipped and will arrive to-morrow morning."

At this exciting juncture of affairs, Mr. McKim, who had been engineering this important undertaking, deemed it expedient to change the programme slightly in one particular at least to insure greater safety. Instead of having a member of the Committee go again to the depot for the box, which might excite suspicion, it was decided that it would be safest to have the express bring it direct to the Anti-Slavery Office.

But all apprehension of danger did not now disappear, for there was no room to suppose that Adams' Express office had any sympathy with the Abolitionist or the fugitive, consequently for Mr. McKim to appear personally at the express office to give directions with reference to the coming of a box from Richmond which would be directed to Arch street, and yet not intended for that street, but for the Anti-Slavery office at 107 North Fifth street, it needed of course no great discernment to foresee that a step of this kind was wholly impracticable and that a more indirect and covert method would have to be adopted. In this dreadful crisis Mr. McKim, with his usual good judgment and remarkably quick, strategical mind, especially in matters pertaining to the U.G.R.R., hit upon the following plan, namely, to go to his friend, E. M. Davis,* who was then extensively engaged in mercantile business, and relate the circumstances. Having daily intercourse with said Adams' Express office, and being well acquainted with the firm and some of the drivers, Mr. Davis could, as Mr. McKim thought, talk about "boxes, freight, etc.," from any part of the country without risk. Mr. Davis heard Mr. McKim's plan and instantly approved of it, and was heartily at his service.

"Dan, an Irishman, one of Adams' Express drivers, is just the fellow to go to the depot after the box," said Davis. "He drinks a little too much whiskey sometimes, but he will do anything I ask him to do, promptly and obligingly. I'll trust Dan, for I believe he is the very man." The difficulty which Mr. McKim had been so anxious to overcome was thus pretty well settled. It was agreed that Dan should go after the box next morning before daylight and bring it to the Anti-Slavery office direct, and to make it all the more agreeable for Dan to get up out of his warm bed and go on this errand before day, it was decided that he should have a five dollar gold piece for himself. Thus these preliminaries having been satisfactorily arranged, it only remained for Mr. Davis to see Dan and give him instructions accordingly, etc.

Next morning, according to arrangement, the box was at the Anti-Slavery office in due time. The witnesses present to behold the resurrection were J. M. McKim, Professor C. D. Cleveland,[40] Lewis Thompson, and the writer.

Mr. McKim was deeply interested; but having been long identified with the Anti-Slavery cause as one of its oldest and ablest advocates in the darkest days of slavery and mobs, and always found by the side of the fugitive to counsel and succor, he was on this occasion perfectly composed.

*[Still's note] E. M. Davis was a member of the Executive Committee of the Pennsylvania Anti-Slavery Society and a long-tried Abolitionist, son-in-law of James and Lucretia Mott.

Professor Cleveland, however, was greatly moved. His zeal and earnestness in the cause of freedom, especially in rendering aid to passengers, knew no limit. Ordinarily he could not too often visit these travelers, shake them too warmly by the hand, or impart to them too freely of his substance to aid them on their journey. But now his emotion was overpowering.

Mr. Thompson, of the firm of Merrihew & Thompson—about the only printers in the city who for many years dared to print such incendiary documents as anti-slavery papers and pamphlets—one of the truest friends of the slave, was composed and prepared to witness the scene.

All was quiet. The door had been safely locked. The proceedings commenced. Mr. McKim rapped quietly on the lid of the box and called out, "All right!" Instantly came the answer from within, "All right, sir!"

The witnesses will never forget that moment. Saw and hatchet quickly had the five hickory hoops cut and the lid off, and the marvellous resurrection of Brown ensued. Rising up in his box, he reached out his hand, saying, "How do you do, gentlemen?" The little assemblage hardly knew what to think or do at the moment. He was about as wet as if he had come up out of the Delaware. Very soon he remarked that, before leaving Richmond he had selected for his arrival-hymn (if he lived) the Psalm beginning with these words: "*I waited patiently for the Lord, and He heard my prayer.*" And most touchingly did he sing the psalm, much to his own relief, as well as to the delight of his small audience.

He was then christened Henry Box Brown, and soon afterwards was sent to the hospitable residence of James Mott[41] and E. M. Davis, on Ninth street, where, it is needless to say, he met a most cordial reception from Mrs. Lucretia Mott and her household. Clothing and creature comforts were furnished in abundance, and delight and joy filled all hearts in that stronghold of philanthropy.

As he had been so long doubled up in the box he needed to promenade considerably in the fresh air, so James Mott put one of his broad-brim hats on his head and tendered him the hospitalities of his yard as well as his house, and while Brown promenaded the yard flushed with victory, great was the joy of his friends.

After his visit at Mr. Mott's, he spent two days with the writer, and then took his departure for Boston, evidently feeling quite conscious of the wonderful feat he had performed, and at the same time it may be safely said that those who witnessed this strange resurrection were not only elated at his success, but were made to sympathize more deeply than ever before with the slave. Also the noble-hearted Smith who boxed him up was made to rejoice over Brown's victory, and was thereby encouraged to render similar service to two other young bondmen, who appealed to him for deliverance. But, unfortunately, in this attempt the undertaking proved a failure. Two boxes containing the young men alluded to above, after having been duly expressed and some distance on the road, were, through the agency of the telegraph, betrayed, and the heroic young fugitives were captured in their boxes and dragged back to hopeless bondage. Consequently, through this deplorable failure, Samuel A. Smith was arrested, imprisoned, and was called upon to suffer severely, as may be seen from the subjoined correspondence, taken from the New York Tribune soon after his release from the penitentiary.

The Deliverer of Box Brown —
Meeting of the Colored Citizens of Philadelphia
[Correspondence of the N.Y. Tribune.]

PHILADELPHIA, Saturday, July 5, 1856.
SAMUEL A. SMITH, who boxed up Henry Box Brown in Richmond, Va., and forwarded him by overland express to Philadelphia, and who was arrested and convicted, eight years ago, for boxing up two other slaves, also directed to Philadelphia, having served out his imprisonment in the Penitentiary, was released on the 18th ultimo,[42] and arrived in this city on the 21st.

Though he lost all his property; though he was refused witnesses on his trial (no officer could be found, who would serve a summons on a witness); though for five long months, in hot weather, he was kept heavily chained in a cell four by eight feet in dimensions; though he received five dreadful stabs, aimed at his heart, by a bribed assassin, nevertheless he still rejoices in the motives which prompted him to "undo the heavy burdens, and let the oppressed go free." Having resided nearly all his life in the South, where he had traveled and seen much of the "peculiar institution," and had witnessed the most horrid enormities inflicted upon the slave, whose cries were ever ringing in his ears, and for whom he had the warmest sympathy, Mr. Smith could not refrain from believing that the black man, as well as the white, had God-given rights. Consequently, he was not accustomed to shed tears when a poor creature escaped from his "kind master;" nor was he willing to turn a deaf ear to his appeals and groans, when he knew he was thirsting for freedom. From 1828 up to the day he was incarcerated, many had sought his aid and counsel, nor had they sought in vain. In various places he operated with success. In Richmond, however, it seemed expedient to invent a new plan for certain emergencies, hence the Box and Express plan was devised, at the instance of a few heroic slaves, who had manifested their willingness to die in a box, on the road to liberty, rather than continue longer under the yoke. But these heroes fell into the power of their enemies. Mr. Smith had not been long in the Penitentiary before he had fully gained the esteem and confidence of the Superintendent and other officers. Finding him to be humane and generous-hearted—showing kindness toward all, especially in buying bread, &c., for the starving prisoners, and by a timely note of warning, which had saved the life of one of the keepers, for whose destruction a bold plot had been arranged— the officers felt disposed to show him such favors as the law would allow. But their good intentions were soon frustrated. The Inquisition (commonly called the Legislature), being in session in Richmond, hearing that the Superintendent had been speaking well of Smith, and circulating a petition for his pardon, indignantly demanded to know if the rumor was well founded. Two weeks were spent by the Inquisition, and many witnesses were placed upon oath, to solemnly testify in the matter. One of the keepers swore that his life had been saved by Smith. Col. Morgan, the Superintendent, frequently testified in writing and verbally to Smith's good deportment; acknowledging that he had circulated petitions, &c.; and took the position, that he sincerely believed, that it would be to the interest of the institution to pardon him; calling the attention of the Inquisition, at the same time, to the fact, that not unfrequently pardons had been granted to criminals, under sentence of death, for the most cold-blooded murder, to say nothing of other gross crimes. The effort for pardon was soon abandoned, for the following reason given by the Governor: "I can't, and I won't pardon him!"

In view of the unparalleled injustice which Mr. S. had suffered, as well as on account of the aid he had rendered to the slaves, on his arrival in this city the colored citizens of Philadelphia felt that he was entitled to sympathy and aid, and straightway invited him to remain a few days, until arrangements could be made for a mass meeting to receive him. Accordingly, on last Monday evening, a mass meeting convened in the Israel church, and the Rev. Wm. T. Catto[43] was called to the chair, and Wm. Still was appointed secretary. The chairman briefly stated the object of the meeting. Having lived in the South, he claimed to know something of the workings of the oppressive system of slavery generally, and declared that, notwithstanding the many exposures of the evil which came under his own observation, the most vivid descriptions fell far short of the realities his own eyes had witnessed. He then introduced Mr. Smith, who arose and in a plain manner briefly told his story, assuring the audience that he had always hated slavery, and had taken great pleasure in helping many out of it, and though he had suffered much physically and pecuniarily for the cause's sake, yet he murmured not, but rejoiced in what he had done. After taking his seat, addresses were made by the Rev. S. Smith, Messrs. Kinnard, Brunner, Bradway, and others. The following preamble and resolutions were adopted—

WHEREAS, We, the colored citizens of Philadelphia, have among us Samuel A. Smith, who was incarcerated over seven years in the Richmond Penitentiary, for doing an act that was honorable to his feelings and his sense of justice and humanity, therefore,

Resolved, That we welcome him to this city as a martyr to the cause of Freedom.

Resolved, That we heartily tender him our gratitude for the good he has done to our suffering race.

Resolved, That we sympathize with him in his losses and sufferings in the cause of the poor, down-trodden slave.

W. S.

During his stay in Philadelphia, on this occasion, he stopped for about a fortnight with the writer, and it was most gratifying to learn from him that he was no new worker on the U.G.R.R. But that he had long hated slavery thoroughly, and although surrounded with perils on every side, he had not failed to help a poor slave whenever the opportunity was presented.

Pecuniary aid, to some extent, was rendered him in this city, for which he was grateful, and after being united in marriage, by Wm. H. Furness, D.D.,[44] to a lady who had remained faithful to him through all his sore trials and sufferings, he took his departure for Western New York, with a good conscience and an unshaken faith in the belief that in aiding his fellow-man to freedom he had but simply obeyed the word of Him who taught man to do unto others as he would be done by.

Notes

1. Originally from Philadelphia, Charles Waln Morgan (1796–1861), a former Quaker, was a whaling businessman in New Bedford, Massachusetts, and was involved in antislavery efforts.

2. William James Rotch (1819–93) was a prominent businessman and politician in New Bedford.

3. "Instant" refers to the current calendar month, so the reference here is to the April 12 issue.

4. Sparta was an ancient city in Greece; the characteristics commonly considered Spartan are simplicity, frugality, courage, or brevity of speech (*Oxford English Dictionary*).

5. Debora Weston—along with her sisters Caroline, Anne, and Maria— was an active and influential abolitionist and one of the founding members of the Boston Female Anti-Slavery Society, created in 1833.

6. On the face of it; at first sight.

7. A theater in Boston available for various events and sometimes used by abolitionists.

8. Wendell Phillips (1811-84) was a Boston lawyer and prominent abolitionist and a supporter of William Lloyd Garrison. He was an active and celebrated speaker and was known for his devotion to various reform movements—woman suffrage, prohibition, and penal reform, among others. Phillips was a leader in the American Anti-Slavery Society and was widely respected by both white and black abolitionists.

9. Frederick Douglass (1818-95) was probably the most prominent and influential African American leader of his time. Born in slavery in Maryland, Douglass became a leading antislavery lecturer, writer, and newspaper editor, founding the *North Star* (1848-51), *Frederick Douglass' Paper* (1851-59), and *Douglass' Monthly* (1860-63). After the Civil War, Douglass held various professional and public offices, including consul general to Haiti (1890-91).

10. William Craft (ca. 1826-1900) and Ellen Craft (1826-91) were married while enslaved and escaped from slavery together in 1848, with Ellen disguised as a young white male slaveholder and William playing the role of her personal slave. Their story was often told in the antislavery press and at public events, and the Crafts published their own version of this escape—*Running a Thousand Miles for Freedom; or, The Escape of William and Ellen Craft from Slavery*—in London in 1860.

11. Douglass acquired the funds to purchase his freedom during his tour of Britain (1845-47), so he was not, at this time, a fugitive slave.

12. John C. Calhoun (1782-1850) of South Carolina was the most prominent southern statesman of his time. An influential political theorist, Calhoun was one of the South's most determined defenders of the system of slavery and an advocate of the doctrine of states' rights.

13. A prominent proslavery advocate, George McDuffie (1790-1851) was a South Carolina legislator, senator, and governor.

14. Edmund Quincy (1808-77) was a white Boston reformer who served as the corresponding secretary of the Massachusetts Anti-Slavery Society from 1844 to 1853.

15. After escaping from slavery in 1834, William Wells Brown (1814-84) became a prominent antislavery lecturer, novelist, dramatist, and historian. His autobiographical narrative, *Narrative of the Life of William W.*

Brown, a Fugitive Slave, Written by Himself, went through numerous editions and helped to establish Brown as one of the most influential black abolitionists in the United States and abroad.

16. Stephen Symonds Foster (1809–81) was an abolitionist and social reformer, husband of the antislavery activist Abby Kelley, and author of *The Brotherhood of Thieves; or, A True Picture of the American Church and Clergy* (1843). He was known for his radical methods, one of which was to interrupt church services to present an antislavery message.

17. Faneuil Hall in Boston, Massachusetts, was the site of many meetings for the American Revolution and became known as the "Cradle of Liberty." Painted portraits of John Quincy Adams, Daniel Webster, Samuel Adams, and John Hancock, among others, were on display there. In the nineteenth century, the hall was often the site of meetings for antislavery and other social reform movements.

18. In their early years, the members of the Massachusetts Anti-Slavery Society had trouble obtaining church or other public space for their convention meetings. According to Elaine Brooks, "A written request, signed by one hundred citizens, was presented to the City Government for the use of Faneuil Hall, but it was denied them. However, on August 21, 1835, Faneuil Hall, which had been refused a few weeks before to the anti-slavery convention, was thrown open to a meeting held for the purpose of protecting slaveholders" ("Massachusetts Anti-Slavery Society," 314).

19. The Mason-Dixon line marked the division of slave and free states at the borders of Pennsylvania in the North and Delaware and Maryland in the South.

20. John Hancock (1737–93) was a merchant who served as the president of the Continental Congress, a signer of the Declaration of Independence, and the first governor of Massachusetts.

21. John Adams (1735–1826) was one of the primary forces in the events leading to the American Revolution, and he served as the second president of the United States. His son John Quincy Adams (1767–1848) was the sixth U.S. president.

22. William Tell is the legendary Swiss leader who opposed Austrian power. The legend first appeared in the fifteenth century. Roland was a legendary figure in medieval Europe, a Christian warrior killed by Muslims in an epic battle.

23. Thomas Babington Macaulay (1800–1859) was an English states-man, essayist, and historian who wrote, among other works, the very popular *History of England from the Accession of James the Second*, the first two volumes of which were published in December 1848 and made Macaulay one of the most popular writers of his time.

24. Elizabeth Gaunt, who was active in dissenting politics in London in the 1680s, was convicted for conspiracy and treason against Charles II and burned to death on October 23, 1685. Following the failure of the Monmouth Rebellion, in which the Duke of Argyll was involved, Elizabeth and her husband William aided fleeing rebels, one of whom betrayed her and contributed to her conviction.

25. Probably a reference to George Jeffreys (1645–89), an English judge known for cruelty. Jeffreys was notorious for his role in the 1685 "Bloody Assizes" that followed the failed insurrection of James Scott, duke of Monmouth. Jeffreys saw to the execution of many of the rebels and ordered that others be sold into slavery in the colonies. When James II was overthrown, Jeffreys disguised himself as a sailor in an unsuccessful attempt to escape. He died in the Tower of London in 1689. In referring to Jeffreys, Phillips is following a consistent line of thought, for Jeffreys was associated with the case of Elizabeth Gaunt, and his infamy was due in part to articles written by Macaulay.

26. Daniel Webster (1782–1852), who represented New Hampshire and, later, Massachusetts in Congress, was one of the most prominent states-men of his time. Webster placed the preservation of the Union above the abolition of slavery and argued against the federal government's right to interfere with the policies of individual states. He would soon become known—indeed, notorious—in abolitionist circles for his support of the Compromise of 1850 and the Fugitive Slave Law that was part of that political compromise.

27. Robert Charles Winthrop (1809–94) was one of the most prominent statesmen of his time. Having studied law with Daniel Webster, he soon entered a political career that included membership in the Massachusetts House of Representatives (1834–40) and the U.S. House of Representatives through most of the 1840s, including the position of Speaker of the House (1847–49). Like Webster, he was known for his oratorical abilities and for his conservative stance on slavery, the Constitution, and the Union.

28. Work on the new Boston Custom House began in 1838, while Win-

throp was serving as the Speaker in the Massachusetts House of Representatives. Webster was the legal adviser for the Boston Associates, a group
of merchant-industrialists interested in consolidating and protecting the
power of the New England textile industry. The Associates built the first
major textile mill in Lowell, Massachusetts.

29. William Lloyd Garrison (1805–79) was the most prominent and influential of the white abolitionists. He established the antislavery newspaper the *Liberator* in 1831. Garrison advocated immediate emancipation
of all slaves; he opposed the Constitution as a "Covenant with Death and
an Agreement with Hell" and advocated secession from the Union.

30. Probably a reference to the Convention of Congregational Ministers of Massachusetts, held in May 1849, which included a moderate and
measured "Report of the Committee on Slavery."

31. Massachusetts sea captain Jonathan Walker (1799–1878) was convicted in 1844 of helping slaves acquire freedom. He served time in jail,
and his hand was branded with the letters "S.S." for "slave stealer," leading
to his fame as "The Man with the Branded Hand."

32. To believe or trust as true.

33. The Boston *Chronotype* was a newspaper founded in 1846 by Elizur
Wright (1804–85). The *Chronotype* was devoted to antislavery, antitariff,
and other political and social reform issues.

34. The Free Soil Party was formed in 1848 by members of various
political parties frustrated by increasing political tensions concerning
slavery. The party's 1848 platform called for an end to slavery in the District of Columbia and an end to its extension in the territories.

35. In Shakespeare's *Othello*, when accused by Brabantio of enchant-
ing Desdemona, Othello begins his defense by promising the Senators, "I
will a round unvarnished tale deliver" (1.3.90). This phrase has often been
used since then to refer to a straightforward account.

36. Famous slave narratives: *Narrative of Henry Watson, a Fugitive Slave*
(1848); *Narrative of the Sufferings of Lewis Clarke, During a Captivity of More
than Twenty-Five Years, Among the Algerines of Kentucky, One of the So Called
Christian States of North America* (1845); *Narrative of William W. Brown, a
Fugitive Slave* (1847); *Narrative of the Life of Frederick Douglass, an American
Slave* (1845); and *The Life of Josiah Henson, Formerly a Slave, Now an Inhabi-
tant of Canada, as Narrated by Himself* (1849).

37. "Cousin Ann" was the pseudonym of Ann Preston (1813–72). The

daughter of a Quaker minister, Preston was a member of the first class to enroll in the Female Medical College of Pennsylvania. In 1853 she became a professor of hygiene and physiology and, in 1866, dean of the renamed Women's Medical College. Reportedly, her family had aided fugitive slaves during her childhood; as an adult, Preston herself was active in antislavery work.

38. In England, Brown's panorama and public appearances were harshly criticized—indeed, ridiculed—by T. H. Brindley, editor of the *Wolverhampton and Staffordshire Herald*. In an 1852 editorial, Brindley called Brown's panorama, "like his oral representation of slavery, . . . a gross and palpable exaggeration" and added that it was "a jumbled mass of contradictions and absurdities, assertions without proof, geography without boundary, and horrors without parallel" (qtd. in Ruggles, *Unboxing*, 143-44). Of Brown himself, Brindley wondered how anyone could approve of the "foppery, conceit, vanity, and egotistical stupidity of the Box Brown school" (qtd. in ibid., 144). Brown brought a legal suit for libel against the *Wolverhampton and Staffordshire Herald* and was awarded damages of one hundred pounds. For the full account of this case, see ibid., 143-45.

39. William Still (1821-1901), one of the most important abolitionists involved in the Underground Railroad, served as secretary and executive director of the General Vigilance Committee in Philadelphia. Out of this work came the records he preserved and published in *The Underground Rail Road*.

40. Charles Dexter Cleveland (1802-69) was a professor of Latin and Greek who published anthologies, poems, essays, and lectures on various subjects. Known for his antislavery sentiments, he served as president of the antislavery society in Philadelphia.

41. James Mott (1788-1868) was a prominent Quaker businessman who, with his influential wife Lucretia Coffin Mott (1793-1880), was active in both the antislavery and the women's rights movements. Together, the couple formed the Philadelphia Free Produce Society to discourage the purchase of products made by slave labor, and they worked together as well to help plan and host the First Woman's Rights Convention in Seneca Falls, New York (1848).

42. Of the previous month.

43. The Reverend William T. Catto had been a slave in South Carolina

but received his freedom and later was ordained a minister. After that, he moved north with his family, eventually settling in Philadelphia.

44. William Henry Furness was the pastor of the First Unitarian Church of Philadelphia. He was known for his strong antislavery sermons and his courageous commitment to the abolitionist cause.

THE TWO NARRATIVES

The version of Brown's narrative presented in this edition was not published in the United States until 2002, when Richard Newman and Henry Louis Gates Jr. offered *Narrative of the Life of Henry Box Brown, Written by Himself* to twenty-first-century readers. This "First English Edition," as it was identified on its title page, was first published in Manchester, England, in 1851. Accordingly, the story of Brown's written account of his life takes us from American antislavery circles to England, where Brown had been compelled to move following threats to his security in the United States (see "Attempt to Kidnap Henry Box Brown" in Appendix B) and especially following the passing of the Fugitive Slave Act of 1850. Brown sailed to England and arrived in Liverpool in November 1851. He immediately commenced a new phase of his antislavery labors and a new stage in his career as a public performer.

By any measure, Brown's approach to his public performances, and to the antislavery cause, was unusual. Marcus Wood, who has called Brown "the most forward-looking of all abolitionist propagandists," notes that Brown "drew on commercial and creative resources which white abolitionists shied away from," and those who have examined Brown's career have remarked on his obvious love of and talent for showmanship.[1] In May 1851, for example, he reenacted his escape and his "resurrection" from the box by having himself shipped from Bradford to Leeds. He continued to present exhibitions featuring his panorama, the *Mirror of Slavery*, and eventually began billing himself as "the African Prince." By 1859 he had remarried, and with his wife's help he launched two panoramas in 1859: the *Grand Original Panorama of African and*

American Slavery, which included "some dioramic views from the Holy Land, which are excellently painted, and ably described by Mrs. H. B. Brown," and a second exhibition concerning "the great Indian Mutiny."[2] By 1859, too, Brown began public presentations dealing in "mesmerism, human magnetism, and electrobiology." After the start of the American Civil War, Brown offered, in 1862, another panorama, the *Grand Moving Mirror of the American War*. By the end of 1863, he was lecturing on electro-biology; these performances involved mesmerism and hypnotic trances. By the time he finally returned to the United States in 1875 with his wife and his daughter Annie, Brown's career had developed to the point where he was performing as a conjurer and a magician and presenting himself as "Prof. H. Box Brown" and offering the "African Prince's Drawing-Room Entertainment."

Through much of this time, and especially throughout the 1850s, Brown was greatly popular throughout England. He traveled across the country, visiting various towns and villages numerous times and to often large and enthusiastic audiences. But his approach to his career was often met with considerable disapproval. The most dramatic criticism came in the form of the 1852 editorials by T. H. Brindley in *Wolverhampton and Staffordshire Herald*, which led to Brown's successful lawsuit against the paper for libel (see the August 27, 1852, letter from *Frederick Douglass' Paper* in Appendix B). To some extent, Brown simply suffered the fate of many African Americans in England as in the United States. As Douglas A. Lorimer observes, "Although Brown gained reparation in this case, neither black speakers nor their subjects were free from ridicule and abuse. In some instances, blacks faced outright discrimination."[3] Brown's flamboyant showmanship made him a particularly conspicuous target for such abuse, and Daphne A. Brooks is quite right to argue that "the episode remains a significant example of how the exhibition and Box Brown's complex network of performance strategies posed a representational crisis to viewers who were seemingly tethered to narrow and troubling racial authenticity politics."[4]

Still, one must note with R. J. M. Blackett that "what is interesting is that not one of the prominent blacks in Britain came to Brown's defense."[5] Indeed, Brown's fellow African Americans in England could be quite critical of Brown's style and practices. James C. A. Smith—the man who had helped Brown escape and who collaborated with him in the preparation and presentation of the panorama—was very public in his criticism in 1851 after Brown broke with him without sharing equally the proceeds from their performances. Among other things, Smith accused Brown of pursuing "a wife in this Country—one of the English fair sex" rather than making attempts to purchase the freedom of the wife and children he left behind in slavery. William Wells Brown, in a letter to white abolitionist Wendell Phillips on September 1, 1852, commented on Brown's successful libel suit but noted as well his own concerns about Brown's public self-presentation. "The editor was certainly to blame," he notes, "yet Brown is a very foolish fellow, to say the least. I saw him some time since, and he had a gold ring on nearly every finger on each hand, and more gold and brass round his neck than would take to hang the bigest [sic] Alderman in London. And as to ruffles about the shirts, he had enough to supply any old maid with cap stuff, for half a century. He had on a green dress coat and white hat, and his whole appearance was that of a well dressed monkey."[6] But it must be noted, too, that Brown was often remembered for such showmanship. Years after seeing him as a child, one Englishman remembered in his autobiography that Brown "used to march through the streets in front of a brass band, clad in a highly-colored and fantastic garb, with an immense drawn sword in his hand."[7] Such techniques drew many people to listen to his message about slavery, racial oppression, and human rights.

Faced with such a controversial figure who worked so far outside the usual expectations for an antislavery lecturer, scholars have not been able to reach a clear consensus as to how Brown's English career should be understood. Audrey Fisch has looked at the ways in which the British public was deeply invested in both praising and criticizing Brown, but she has suggested that personal profit was always prominent among Brown's many motives. She has commented on "Brown's success in commodifying his sufferings for display in front of English strangers, in combining celebration of spectacle with English nationalism, but also in catering to the racism of that nationalism."[8] Brooks similarly notes the various motives that might have driven Brown's public performances but suggests that much of the criticism is revealing about the assumptions and perspectives of those in the antislavery movement. "Simply put," Brooks argues, "in the end, Brown's brash and spectacular public acts may have indeed proved too excessive, too performative, too 'glam' to register as legible acts of social and political resistance to slavery."[9] Whatever one might make of Brown's approaches to his performances, though, one can hardly ignore the considerable challenges Brown faced in establishing himself and his life on his own terms after escaping from slavery and after resettling in England. It is as Ruggles has observed: "Brown's status as a fugitive slave was no longer his primary identity. He had become H. Box Brown, a professional performer with a variety of talents. He was the African prince. He was the King of all Mesmerizers. He was who he had made himself to be."[10]

Being who he made himself to be was no small task. Those who escaped from slavery and were assisted in moving to England found themselves in a culture of demanding and often narrow benevolence. Wood has summarized the general situation in which many of the formerly enslaved found themselves upon their arrival in England. "The British Anti-Slavery Society," Wood notes, "had narrow ideas about how it expected black ex-slave lecturers to behave and publicise their experiences. Black abolitionists had to arrive with letters of introduction from white Northern abolitionists and were expected to present themselves as sober Christians intent on bettering themselves in white society. They were even encouraged to move on to work as missionaries in Africa, and several American ex-slaves took this option."[11] Brown's attempt to go his own way, and on his own terms, then, was hardly surprising and could be viewed as both courageous and culturally significant. As Wood puts it, "Henry Box Brown appears . . . to have kicked against the pricks and to have been very much his own man. He delighted in showmanship, and in the performance of his escape."[12] Viewing his career from this angle, one might say that Brown turned showmanship into a second emancipation, or perhaps a series of ongoing acts of liberation and independence, a shifting performance in a shifty, constricting, and even threatening world.

Such performative strategies are exactly the point in considering the shift in tone, presentation, and rhetorical strategies from the 1849 *Narrative of Henry Box Brown, Who Escaped from Slavery Enclosed in a Box 3 Feet Long and 2 Wide. Written from a Statement of Facts Made by Himself, With Remarks Upon the Remedy for Slavery*, written by Charles Stearns, to the 1851 *Narrative of the Life of Henry Box Brown*, which includes in its title the significant phrase "Written by Himself." As I have explained in the introduction to this edition, Brown's most diligent biographer has observed that "although the 1851 *Narrative* is more directly Brown's expression than the 1849 *Narrative*, Brown did not put the words on paper."[13] Who helped Brown write this narrative—and whether it was one person or many—is unknown. Ruggles argues that internal evidence indicates that the *Narrative* was written before Brown arrived in England, and that English friends or allies helped to edit and publish the manuscript. However, the details presented in the narrative, the overall rhetorical strategy of the narrative, and the arrangement of some of Brown's most important performance pieces from his public appearances all make it clear that there is reason to accept the phrase "written by himself" as a sign of Brown's authorship of this edition. "Whether literally authored by the activist or not," Brooks argues, the 1851 *Narrative* "distinguishes itself as an intertextual cultural production, a narrative which finally and emphatically affirms Brown's use of performative strategies to transcend the corporeal as well as the discursive restrictions laid upon him as a fugitive slave."[14] Brown's *Narrative*, in short, was part of Brown's overall self-creation, his attempt to define both himself and his cause beyond the usual protocols of the transatlantic antislavery movement.

Certainly, the most dramatic change is the removal of Charles Stearns's often overbearing presence in the 1849 *Narrative*. In that earlier version, Stearns does not simply put elaborate rhetoric in Brown's mouth; he also has Brown introduce Stearns himself as someone more capable of speaking against the legal injustices of the system of slavery. More broadly, in the 1849 *Narrative* Brown often seems to be simply the occasion for Stearns's own anti-slavery manifesto, presented in the form of a treatise titled "Cure for the Evil of Slavery," for which Brown's own story seems but an elaborate introduction. But Stearns is not completely absent from the 1851 *Narrative*, for the "first English edition" was not a complete rewriting of the 1849 version. Traces of Stearns's rhetoric still remain, and the overall pattern of many of the episodes related in the narrative still follow the lead of the collaborative efforts of Stearns and Brown in 1849. But the changes are dramatic nonetheless, and readers of the 1849 *Narrative* will appreciate the extent to which Brown has, in effect, liberated himself from Stearns's presence.

What follows is a sampling of Stearns's presentation of the 1849 *Narrative*, offered here so that readers can acquire a sense of the significant differences between the two narratives, and also so that readers can sense the traces of the rhetorical tone of the earlier narrative in the 1851 version.

Charles Stearns's Preface

Not for the purpose of administering to a prurient desire to "hear and see some new thing,"[15] nor to gratify any inclination on the part of the hero of the following story to be honored by man, is this simple and touching narrative of the perils of a seeker after the "boon of liberty," introduced to the public eye; but that the people of this country may be made acquainted with the horrid sufferings endured by one as, in a *portable prison*, shut out from the light of heaven, and nearly deprived of its balmy air, he pursued his fearful journey directly through the heart of a country making its boasts of liberty and freedom to all, and that thereby a chord of human sympathy may be touched in the hearts of those who listen to his plaintive tale, which may be the means of furthering the spread of those principles, which under God, shall yet prove "mighty to the pulling down of the strong-holds"[16] of slavery.

O reader, as you peruse this heart-rending tale, let the tear of sympathy roll freely from your eyes, and let the deep fountains of human feeling, which God has implanted in the breast of every son and daughter of Adam, burst forth from their enclosure, until a stream shall flow therefrom on to the surrounding world, of so invigorating and purifying a nature, as to arouse from the "death of the sin"[17] of slavery, and cleanse from the pollutions thereof, all with whom you may be connected. As Henry Box Brown's thrilling escape is portrayed before you, let it not be perused by you as an idle tale, while you go away "forgetting what manner of persons you are;"[18] but let truth find an avenue through your sensibilities, by which it can reach the citadel of your soul, and there dwell in all its life-giving power, expelling the whole brotherhood of pro-slavery errors, which politicians, priests, and selfish avarice, have introduced to the acquaintance of your intellectual faculties. These faculties are oftener blinded by selfishness, than are imbecile of themselves, as the powerful intellect of a Webster is led captive to the inclinations of a not unselfish heart; so that that which should be the ruling power of every man's nature, is held in degrading submission to the inferior feelings of his heart. If man is blinded to the appreciation of the good, by a mass of selfish sensibilities, may he not be induced to surrender his will to the influence of truth, by *benevolent* feelings being caused to spring forth in his heart? That this may be the case with all whose eyes gaze upon the picture here drawn of misery, and of endurance, worthy of a Spartan, and such as a hero of olden times might be proud of, and transmit to posterity, along with the armorial emblazonry of his ancestors, is the ardent desire of all connected with the publication of this work. A word in regard to the literary character of the tale before you. The narrator is freshly from a land where books and schools are forbidden under severe penalties, to all in his former condition, and of course knoweth not letters, having never learned them; but of his capabilities otherwise, no one can doubt, when they recollect that if the records of all nations, from the time when Adam and Eve first placed their free feet upon the soil of Eden, until the conclusion of the scenes depicted by Hildreth[19] and Macaulay, should be diligently searched, a parallel instance of heroism, in behalf of personal liberty, could not be found. Instances of fortitude for the defence of religious freedom, and in cases of a violation of conscience being required; and for the sake of offspring, of friends and of one's country are not uncommon; but whose heroism and ability to contrive, united, have equalled our friend's whose story is now before you?*

A William and an Ellen Craft, indeed performed an almost equally hazardous undertaking, and one which, as a devoted admirer of human daring has said, far exceeded any thing recorded by Macaulay, and will yet be made the ground-work for a future Scott[20] to build a more intensely interesting tale upon than "the author of Waverly" ever put forth, but they had the benefit of their eyes and ears—they were not entirely helpless; enclosed in a moving tomb, and as utterly destitute of power to control your movements as if death had fastened its icy arm upon you, and yet possessing all the full tide of gushing sensibilities, and a complete knowledge of your existence, as was the case with our friend. We read with horror of the burial of persons before life has entirely fled from them, but here is a man who voluntarily assumed a condition in which he well knew all the chances were against him, and when his head seemed well-nigh severed from his body, on account of the concussion occasioned by the rough handling to which he was subject, see the Spartan firmness of his soul. Not a groan escaped from his agonized heart, as the realities of his condition were so vividly presented before him. Death stared him in the face, but like Patrick Henry, only when the alternative was more a matter of fact than it was to that patriot, he exclaims, "Give me liberty or give me death;" and death seemed to say, as quickly as the lion seizes the kid cast into its den, "You are already mine," and was about to wrap its sable mantle around the form of our self-martyred hero—bound fast upon the altars of freedom, as the Hindoo widow is bound upon the altar of a husband's love;[21] when the bright angel of liberty, whose dazzling form he had so

*[Stearns's note] HUGO GROTIUS was, in the year 1620, sent from prison, confined in a small chest of drawers, by the affectionate hands of a faithful wife, but he was taken by *friends* on horseback and carried to the house of a friend, without undergoing much suffering or running the terrible risk which our friend ran.

long and so anxiously watched, as he pored over the scheme hid in the recesses of his own fearless brain, while yet a slave, and whose shining eyes had bewitched his soul, until he had said in the language of one of old to Jesus, "I will follow thee whithersoever thou goest;"[22] when this blessed goddess stood at his side, and, as Jesus said to one lying cold in death's embrace, "I say unto thee, arise,"[23] said to him, as she took him by the hand and lifted him from his travelling tomb, "thy warfare is over, thy work is accomplished, a free man art thou, my guidance has availed thee, arise and breathe the air of freedom."[24]

Did Lazarus[25] astonish his weeping sisters, and the surrounding multitude, as he emerged from his house of clay, clad in the habiliments of the grave, and did joy unfeigned spread throughout that gazing throng? How much more astonishing seemed the birth of Mr. Brown, as he "came forth" from a box, clothed not in the habiliments of the grave, but in those of slavery, worse than the "silent house of death," as his acts had testified; and what greater joy thrilled through the wondering witnesses, as the lid was removed from the travelling carriage of our friend's electing, and straightway arose therefrom a living man, a being made in God's own image, a son of Jehovah, whom the piety and republicanism of this nation had doomed to pass through this terrible ordeal, before the wand of the goddess of liberty could complete his transformation from a slave to a free man! But we will desist from further comments. Here is the plain narrative of our friend, and is it asking too much of you, whose sympathies may be aroused by the recital which follows, to continue to peruse these pages until the cause of all his sufferings is depicted before you, and your duty under the circumstances is clearly pointed out?

Beginning of the 1849 Narrative

I AM not about to harrow the feelings of my readers by a terrific representation of the untold horrors of that fearful system of oppression, which for thirty-three long years entwined its snaky folds about my soul, as the serpent of South America[26] coils itself around the form of its unfortunate victim. It is not my purpose to descend deeply into the dark and noisome caverns of the hell of slavery, and drag from their frightful abode those lost spirits who haunt the souls of the poor slaves, daily and nightly with their frightful presence, and with the fearful sound of their terrific instruments of torture; for other pens far abler than mine have effectually performed that portion of the labor of an exposer of the enormities of slavery. Slavery, like the shield discovered by the knights of olden time, has two diverse sides to it; the one, on which is fearfully written in letters of blood, the character of the mass who carry on that dreadful system of unhallowed bondage; the other, touched with the pencil of a gentler delineator, and telling the looker on, a tale of comparative freedom, from the terrible deprivations so vividly portrayed on its opposite side.

My book will present, if possible, the beautiful side of the picture of slavery; will entertain you with stories of partial kindness on the part of my master, and of comparative enjoyment on my own part, as I grew up under the benign influence of the blessed system so closely connected with our "republican institutions," as Southern politicians tell us.

From the time I first breathed the air of human existence, until the hour of my escape from bondage, I did not receive but one whipping. I never suffered from lack of food, or on account of too extreme labor; nor for want of sufficient clothing to cover my person. My tale is not, therefore, one of horrid inflictions of the lash upon my naked body; of cruel starvings and of insolent treatment; but is the very best representation of slavery which can be given; therefore, reader, allow me to inform you, as you, for aught I know, may be one of those degraded mortals who fancy that if no blows are inflicted upon the slave's body, and a plenty of "bread and bacon" is dealed out to him, he is therefore no sufferer, and slavery is not a cruel institution; allow me to inform you, that I did not escape from such deprivations. It was not for fear of the lash's dreaded infliction, that I endured that fearful imprisonment, which you are waiting to read concerning; nor because of destitution of the necessaries of life, did I enclose myself in my travelling prison, and traverse your boasted land of freedom, a portion of the time with my head in an inverted position, as if it were a terrible crime for me to endeavor to escape from slavery.

Far beyond, in terrible suffering, all outward cruelties of the foul system, are those inner pangs which rend the heart of fond affection, when the "bone of your bone, and the flesh of your flesh" is separated from your embrace, by the ruthless hand of the merciless tyrant, as he plucks from your heart of love, the one whom God hath given you for a "help-meet" through the journey of life; and more fearful by far than all the blows of the bloody lash, or the pangs of cruel hunger are those lashings of the *heart*, which the best of slaveholders inflict upon their happy and "well off" slaves, as they tear from their grasp the pledges of love, smiling at the side of devoted attachment. Tell me not of kind masters under slavery's hateful rule! There is no such thing as a person of that description; for, as you will see, my master, one of the most distinguished of this uncommon class of slaveholders, hesitated not to allow the wife of my love to be torn from my fond embrace, and the darling idols of my heart, my little children, to be snatched from my arms, and thus to doom them to a separation from me, more dreadful to all of us than a large number of lashes, inflicted on us daily. And yet to this fate I was continually subject, during a large portion of the time, when heaven *seemed* to smile propitiously above me; and no black clouds of fearful character lowered over my head. Heaven save me from kind masters, as well as from those called more cruel; for even their "tender mercies are cruel," and what no freeman could endure for a moment. My tale necessarily lacks that thrilling interest which is attached to the more than romantic, although perfectly true descriptions of a life in slavery, given by my numerous forerunners in the work of sketching a slave's personal experience; but I shall endeavor to intermingle with it other scenes which came under my own observation, which will serve to convince you, that if I was spared a worse fate than actually fell to my lot, yet my comrades around me were not so fortunate; but were the victims of the ungovernable rage of those men, of whose characters one cannot be informed, without experiencing within his soul, a rushing of overflowing emotions of pity, indignation and horror.

I first drew the breath of life in Louisa County, Va., forty-five miles from the city of Richmond, in the year 1816. I was born a slave. Not because at the moment of my birth an angel stood by, and declared that such was the will of God concerning me; although in a country whose most honored writings declare that all men have a right to liberty, given them by their Creator, it seems strange that I, or any of my brethren, could have been born without this inalienable right, unless God had thus signified his departure from his usual rule, as described by our fathers. Not, I say, on account of God's willing it to be so, was I born a slave, but for the reason that nearly all the people of this country are united in legislating against heaven, and have contrived to vote down our heavenly father's rules, and to substitute for them, that cruel law which binds the chains of slavery upon one sixth part of the inhabitants of this land. I was born a slave! and wherefore? Tyrants, remorseless, destitute of religion and principle, stood by the couch of my mother, as heaven placed a pure soul, in the infantile form, there lying in her arms—a new being, never having breathed earth's atmosphere before; and fearlessly, with no compunctions of remorse, stretched forth their bloody arms and pressed the life of God from me, baptizing my soul and body as their own property; goods and chattels in their hands! Yes, they robbed me of myself, before I could know the nature of their wicked acts; and for ever afterwards, until I took possession of my own soul and body, did they retain their stolen property. This was why I was born a slave. Reader, can you understand the horrors of that fearful name? Listen, and I will assist you in this difficult work. My father, and my *mother* of course,[27] were slaves before me; but both of them are now enjoying the invaluable boon of liberty, having purchased themselves, in this land of freedom! At an early age, my mother would take me on her knee, and pointing to the forest trees adjacent, now being stripped of their thick foliage by autumnal winds, would say to me, "my son, as yonder leaves are stripped from off the trees of the forest, so are the children of slaves swept away from them by the hands of cruel tyrants;" and her voice would tremble, and she would seem almost choked with her deep emotions, while the big tears would find their way down her saddened cheeks, as she fondly pressed me to her heaving bosom, as if to save me from so dreaded a calamity. I was young then, but I well recollect the sadness of her countenance, and the mournfulness of her words, and they made a deep impression upon my youthful mind. Mothers of the North, as you gaze upon the free forms of your idolized little ones, as they playfully and confidently move around you, O if you knew that the lapse of a few years would infallibly remove them from your affectionate care, not to be laid in the silent grave, "where the wicked cease from troubling," but to be the sport of cruel men, and the victims of barbarous tyrants, who would snatch them from your side, as the robber seizes upon the bag of gold in the traveller's hand; O, would not your life then be rendered a miserable one indeed? Who can trace the workings of a slave mother's soul, as she counts over the hours, the departure of which, she almost knows, will rob her of her darling children, and consign them to a fate more horrible than death's cold embrace! O, who can hear of these cruel deprivations, and not be aroused to action in the slave's behalf?

Brown's Plan to Escape

But you are eager to learn the particulars of my journey from freedom to liberty. The first thing that occurred to me, after the cruel separation of my wife and children from me, and I had recovered my senses, so as to know how to act, was, thoughts of freeing myself from slavery's iron yoke. I had suffered enough under its heavy weight, and I determined I would endure it no longer; and those reasons which often deter the slave from attempting to escape, no longer existed in reference to me, for my family were gone, and slavery now had no mitigating circumstances, to lessen the bitterness of its cup of woe. It is true, as my master had told me, that I could "get another wife;" but no man, excepting a brute below the human species, would have proposed such a step to a person in my circumstances; and as I was not such a degraded being, I did not dream of so conducting. Marriage was not a thing of personal convenience with me, to be cast aside as a worthless garment, whenever the slaveholder's will required it; but it was a sacred institution binding upon me, as long as the God who had "joined us together," refrained from untying the nuptial knot. What! leave the wife of my bosom for another! and while my heart was leaping from its abode, to pour its strong affections upon the kindred soul of my devoted partner, could I receive a stranger, another person to my embrace, as if the ties of love existed only in the presence of the object loved! Then, indeed, should I have been a traitor to that God, who had linked our hearts together in fond affection, and cemented our union, by so many additional cords, twining around our hearts; as a tree and an arbor are held together by the clinging of the tendrils of the adhering vine, which winds itself about them so closely. Slavery, and slavery abettors, seize hold of these tender scions, and cut and prune them away from both tree and arbor, as remorselessly as a gardener cuts down the briars and thorns which disturb the growth of his fair plants; but all humane, and every virtuous man, must instinctively recoil from such transactions, as they would from soul murder, or from the commission of some enormous deed of villany.

Reader, in the light of these scenes you may behold, as in a glass, your true character. Refined and delicate you may pretend to be, and may pass yourself off as a pure and virtuous person; but if you refuse to exert yourself for the overthrow of a system, which thus tramples human affection under its bloody feet, and demands of its crushed victims, the sacrifice of all that is noble, virtuous and pure, upon its smoking altars; you may rest assured, that if the balances of *purity* were extended before you, He who "searcheth the hearts, and trieth the reins,"[28] would say to you, as your character underwent his searching scrutiny, "Thou art weighed in the balance and found wanting."[29]

I went to Mr. Allen, and requested of him permission to refrain from labor for a short time, in consequence of a disabled finger; but he refused to grant me this permission, on the ground that my hand was not lame enough to justify him in so doing. Nothing daunted by this rebuff, I took some oil of vitriol, intending to pour a few drops upon my finger, to make it sufficiently sore, to disable me from work, which I succeeded in, beyond my wishes; for in my hurry, a larger quantity than it was my purpose to apply to my finger, found its way there, and my finger was soon eaten through to the bone. The overseer then was obliged to allow me to absent myself from business, for it was impossible for me to work in that situation. But I did not waste my precious furlough in idle mourning over my fate. I armed myself with determined energy, for action, and in the words of one of old, in the name of God, "I leaped over a wall, and run through a troop"[30] of difficulties. After searching for assistance for some time, I at length was so fortunate as to find a friend, who promised to assist me, for one half the money I had about me, which was one hundred and sixty-six dollars. I gave him eighty-six, and he was to do his best in forwarding my scheme. Long did we remain together, attempting to devise ways and means to carry me away from the land of separation of families, of whips and thumbscrews, and auction blocks; but as often as a plan was suggested by my friend, there would appear some difficulty in the way of its accomplishment. Perhaps it may not be best to mention what these plans were, as some unfortunate slaves may thereby be prevented from availing themselves of these methods of escape.

At length, after praying earnestly to Him, who seeth afar off, for assistance, in my difficulty, suddenly, as if from above, there darted into my mind these words, "Go and get a box, and put yourself in it." I pondered the words over in my mind. "Get, a box?" thought I; "what can this mean?" But I was "not disobedient unto the heavenly vision," and I determined to put into practice this direction, as I considered it, from my heavenly Father.** I went to the depot, and there noticed the size of the largest boxes, which commonly were sent by the cars, and returned with their dimensions. I then repaired to a carpenter, and induced him to make me a box of such a description as I wished, informing him of the use I intended to make of it. He assured me I could not live in it; but as it was dear liberty I was in pursuit of, I thought it best to make the trial.

When the box was finished, I carried it, and placed it before

**[Stearns's note] Reader, smile not at the above idea, for if there is a God of love, we must believe that he suggests steps to those who apply to him in times of trouble, by which they can be delivered from their difficulty. I firmly believe this doctrine, and know it to be true from frequent experience. C. S.

my friend, who had promised to assist me, who asked me if that was to "put my clothes in?" I replied that it was not, but to "*put Henry Brown in!*" He was astonished at my temerity; but I insisted upon his placing me in it, and nailing me up, and he finally consented.

After corresponding with a friend in Philadelphia, arrangements were made for my departure, and I took my place in this narrow prison, with a mind full of uncertainty as to the result. It was a critical period of my life, I can assure you, reader; but if you have never been deprived of your liberty, as I was, you cannot realize the power of that hope of freedom, which was to me indeed, "an anchor to the soul, sure and steadfast."[31]

I laid me down in my darkened home of three feet by two, and like one about to be guillotined,[32] resigned myself to my fate. My friend was to accompany me, but he failed to do so; and contented himself with sending a telegraph message to his correspondent in Philadelphia, that such a box was on its way to his care.

Stearns's "Cure for the Evil of Slavery"

[At the end of the narrative, Stearns has Brown lead into Stearns's treatise the "Cure for the Evil of Slavery." Most of the "Cure for the Evil of Slavery" is an extended discussion of the conditions and justifications that led to the American Revolution as related to the antislavery cause, and especially to Stearns's call for "a new government at the North." What is included here is the end of the *Narrative* proper, at which point Brown introduces the reader to Stearns, and then the beginning of Stearns's roughly twenty-five-page treatise (close to a third of the 1849 *Narrative*).]

I now stand before you as a free man, but since my arrival among you, I have been informed that your laws require that I should still be held as a slave; and that if my master should espy me in any nook or corner of the free states, according to the constitution of the United States, he could secure me and carry me back into Slavery; so that I am confident I am not safe, even here, if what I have heard concerning your laws is true. I cannot imagine why you should uphold such strange laws. I have been told that every time a man goes to the polls and votes, he virtually swears to sustain them, frightful as they are. It seems to me to be a hard case, for a man to endure what I have endured in effecting my escape, and then to be continually exposed to be seized by my master, and carried back into that horrid pit from which I have escaped. I have been told, however, that the people here would not allow me to be thus returned, that they would break their own laws in my behalf, which seems quite curious to me; for why should you make laws, and swear to uphold them, and then break them? I do not understand much about laws, to be sure, as the law of my master is the one I have been subject to all my life, but some how, it looks a little singular to me, that wise people should be obliged to break their own laws, or else do a very wicked act. I have been told that there are twice as many voters at the North as there are at the South, and much more wealth, as well as other things of importance, which makes me study much, why the Northern people live under such laws. If I was one of them, and had any influence among them, it appears to me, I should advocate the overthrow of such laws, and the establishment of better ones in their room. Many people tell me besides, that if the slaves should rise up, and do as they did in Nat Turner's time, endeavor to fight their way to freedom, that the Northern people are pledged to shoot them down, and keep them in subjection to their masters. Now I cannot understand this, for almost all the people tell me, that they "are opposed to Slavery," and yet they swear to prevent the slaves from obtaining their liberty! If these things could be made clear to my mind, I should be glad; but a fog hangs over my eyes at present in reference to this matter.

I now wish to introduce to your hearing a friend of mine, who will tell you more about these things than I can, until I have had more time to examine this curious subject. What he shall have to say to you, may not be as interesting as the account of my sufferings, but if you really wish to help my brethren in bondage, you will not be unwilling to hear what he may say to you, in reference to the way to abolish slavery, as you cannot be opposed to my sufferings, unless you are willing to exert yourselves for the overthrow of the cruel system which caused them.

Dear Friends,—You have listened with eager ears, and with tearful eyes, to the recital of Mr. Brown. He has alluded to the laws which many of you uphold, when you go to the polls and vote, but he has not informed you of your duty at the present crisis. What I have to say at this time, will be mainly directed to the remedy for this terrible evil, so strikingly portrayed in his eventful life. As one of those who desire the abolition of Slavery, it is my earnest desire to be made acquainted with a true and proper remedy for this dreadful disease. I apprehend that no moral evil exists, for the cure of which there cannot be found some specific, the application of which, will effectually eradicate the disorder. I am not a politician, and cannot write as politicians do. Still I may be pardoned for entering a little into their sphere of action, for the purpose of plucking some choice fruit from the overhanging boughs of that fruitful arena. I am not *afraid* of politics, for I do not regard them as too sacred, or as too profane, for me to handle. I believe that the people of this country are not ready for a truly Christian government; therefore, although I cannot unite myself with any other, yet I should be rejoiced, at beholding the faintest resemblance to such an one, in opposition to our present proslavery government.

I would like to see all men perfect Christians, but as I do not expect to witness this sight very soon, I am gratified at their becoming anti-slavery, or even temperance men. Any advance from the old corruptions of the past, is hailed with delight by me.

The point I would now urge upon your attention is, the immediate formation of *a new government at the North*, at all events, and at all hazards! I do not say, "Down with this Union" merely, but I do say, up with an Anti-Slavery government, in the free States. Our object should be the establishment of a form of government, directly in opposition to the one we at present live under. The stars and stripes of our country's flag, should be trodden into the dust, and a white banner, with the words, "Emancipation to the Slaves" inscribed upon it, should be unfurled to the breeze, in the room of the old emblem of despotic servitude. Too long have we been dilatory upon this point; but the period I believe has now arrived, for us to strike for freedom, in earnest. Let us see first, what we have to accomplish; and then the means whereby we can bring about the desired end; our capabilities for such a work; and the reasons why we should adopt this plan; and what will be the consequences of such a course of action. First. What have we to accomplish? A great and an important end truly, which is nothing less, than the establishment of a new government, right in the midst of our present pro-slavery one.

A government, is a system of authority sustained by either the rulers, or the ruled, or by both conjointly. If it depends on the will of the rulers, then they can change it at pleasure; but if the people are connected with it, their consent must be gained, before its character can be altered. If, as is the case with our government, it is the *people* who "ordain and establish" laws, then it lies with them to change those laws, and to remodel that government. Let this fact be distinctly understood; for the majority of the people of this land, seem to labor under the delusion, that our government is sustained by some other power than their own; and are very much in the situation of those heathen nations, condemned by one of the ancient prophets, who manufactured their deities, and then fell down and worshipped the work of their own hands. The people make laws for their own guidance, and then offer as an excuse for their bad conduct, that the *laws* require them to do so! The government appears to be yet surrounded with a halo of glory, as it was in the days of kingly authority, when "the powers that be" were supposed to have been approvingly "ordained of God," and men fear to touch the sacred structure of their own erecting, as if God's throne would be endangered thereby. This is not the only manifestation of self-esteem connected with their movements.

The people also fancy, that what their fathers created is divine, when their fathers have departed, and left them to do as they elect, without any obligation resting upon them to follow in their steps; but so great is the self-esteem of the people, as manifested in their pride of ancestry, that they seem to suppose, that God would cast them off forever, if they should cease to be children, and become men, casting from them, the doctrines and political creeds of their fathers; and yet they boast of their spirit of progress! They fear to act for themselves, lest they should mar the reputation of their ancestors, and be deprived of their feeling of self-adulation, in consequence of the perfection of their worthy sires. But we must humble our pride, and cease worshipping, either our own, or our father's handiwork, — in reference to the laws, of which we are speaking. What we want is, a very simple thing. Our fathers proclaimed themselves free and independent of the British government, and proceeded to establish a new one, in its room. They threw off the British yoke! We can do the same, in reference to the United States government! We can put forth *our* "declaration of independence," and issue our manifesto of grievances; and as our fathers did, can pledge to one another, "our lives, our property and our sacred honor,"[33] in promoting the accomplishment of this end. We can *immediately organize* a new government, independent of the present one under which we live. We may be deemed traitors for so doing; but were not Samuel Adams[34] and John Hancock traitors? and did not our forefathers inscribe on their banners, "resistance to tyrants is obedience to God?"[35] Are we more faint-hearted than they were? Are not our and the slave's grievances more unendurable than were their wrongs? A new government is what we want; and the sound should go forth from all these free hills, echoing across the plains of the far distant West, that New England and the whole North, are ready to do battle with the myrmidons of the slave power, not with the sword of steel, but with the spirit of patient submission to robbery and death, in defence of our principles. We are not obliged to muster our squadrons in "hot haste," to the "sound of the cannon's deafening roar," nor to arm ourselves for physical combat; for there is more power in suffering death, for truth's sake, than in fighting with swords of steel, and with cannon balls. A new government we must have.

Notes

1. Wood, *Blind Memory*, 116, 107.
2. Ruggles, *Unboxing*, 152.

3. Lorimer, *Colour, Class and the Victorians*, 54.

4. Brooks, *Bodies in Dissent*, 95.

5. Blackett, *Building an Antislavery Wall*, 159.

6. Qtd. in Ruggles, *Unboxing*, 145.

7. Ibid., 151.

8. Fisch, *American Slaves*, 81.

9. Brooks, *Bodies in Dissent*, 130.

10. Ruggles, *Unboxing*, 159.

11. Wood, *Blind Memory*, 106.

12. Ibid.

13. Ruggles, *Unboxing*, 129.

14. Brooks, *Bodies in Dissent*, 126.

15. The phrase refers to the Bible, Acts 17:21: "For all the Athenians, and strangers which were there, spent their time in nothing else, but either to tell or to hear some new thing." The verse refers to those who value learning over truth, always looking for something new or intellectually fashionable, valuing learning for its own sake rather than as a means to attain wisdom.

16. This phrase appears regularly in Christian commentary, and is based on the Bible, 2 Cor. 3-6: "For though we walk in the flesh, we do not war after the flesh: (For the weapons of our warfare *are* not carnal, but mighty through God to the pulling down of strongholds;) Casting down imaginations, and every high thing that exalteth itself against the knowledge of God, and bringing into captivity every thought to the obedience of Christ; And having in a readiness to revenge all disobedience, when your obedience is fulfilled."

17. This phrase appears regularly in Christian commentary and refers to the new birth of Christian believers, as presented in the Bible, Rom. 6: 1–11:

What shall we say then? Shall we continue in sin, that grace may abound? God forbid. How shall we, that are dead to sin, live any longer therein? Know ye not, that so many of us as were baptized into Jesus Christ were baptized into his death? Therefore we are buried with him by baptism into death: that like as Christ was raised up from the dead by the glory of the Father, even so we also should walk in newness of life. For if we have been planted together in the likeness of his death, we shall be also *in the likeness* of *his* resurrection: Knowing this, that our old man is crucified with *him*, that the body of sin might be destroyed, that henceforth we should not serve sin. For he that is dead is freed from sin. Now if we be dead with Christ, we believe that we shall also live with him: Knowing that Christ being raised from the dead dieth no more; death hath no more dominion over him. For in that he died, he died unto sin once; but in that he liveth, he liveth unto God. Likewise reckon ye also yourselves to be dead indeed unto sin, but alive unto God through Jesus Christ our Lord.

18. The phrase refers to the necessity of Christian remembrance and steadfastness, and is drawn from the Bible, 2 Pet. 3:11-12: "*Seeing* then *that* all these things shall be dissolved, what manner *of persons* ought ye to be in *all* holy conversation and godliness, Looking for and hasting unto the coming of the day of God, wherein the heavens being on fire shall be dissolved, and the elements shall melt with fervent heat?"

19. Richard Hildreth (1807-65) was an American historian and social commentator who was opposed to slavery. Among his various publications are one of the first antislavery novels (first published anonymously and imagined by some to be an actual slave narrative), *The Slave; or, Memoirs of Archie Moore* (1836), and the six-volume *History of the United States* (1849-52), in both of which his antislavery sentiments were clear.

20. Sir Walter Scott (1771-1832), a British poet and novelist, was a popular and respected writer whose influence in American literature and culture was enormous. His first novel, which launched a series of historical fiction, was *Waverly; or 'Tis Sixty Years Since* (1814).

21. Hindu women were sometimes burned on an altar following their husbands' deaths, and images or tales of such burnings were widely circulated in European and American culture in the nineteenth century.

22. From the Bible, Matt. 8:19: "And a certain scribe came, and said unto him, Master, I will follow thee whithersoever thou goest." See also Luke 9:57.

23. From the Bible, Luke 5:18-25:

And, behold, men brought in a bed a man which was taken with a palsy: and they sought *means* to bring him in, and to lay *him* before him. And when they could not find by what *way* they might bring him in because of the multitude, they went upon the housetop, and let him down through the tiling with *his* couch into the midst before Jesus. And when he saw their faith, he said unto him, Man, thy sins are forgiven thee. And the scribes and the Pharisees began to reason, saying, Who is this which speaketh blasphemies? Who can forgive sins, but God alone? But when Jesus perceived their thoughts, he answering said unto them, What reason ye in your hearts? Whether is easier, to say, Thy sins be forgiven thee; or to say, Rise up and walk? But that ye may know that the Son of man hath power upon earth to forgive sins, (he said unto the sick of the palsy,) I say unto thee, Arise, and take up thy couch, and go into thine house. And immediately he rose up before them, and took up that whereon he lay, and departed to his own house, glorifying God.

24. The phrase "thy warfare o're" is from Walter Scott's poem *The Lady of the Lake* (1810) and appeared as well in folk songs, usually about the death of soldiers.

25. A reference to the Bible, John 11, in which Jesus raises Lazarus from the dead.

26. Probably simply the southern states of the United States.

27. This phrase appears in the 1851 version of the *Narrative*, but without the comma before "and my mother" and without the added emphasis on "mother." The emphasis here refers to the fact that children followed the condition of the mother, so that children of an enslaved mother were themselves enslaved, regardless of the condition or race of the father.

28. A reference to the Bible, Rev. 2:23: "And I will kill her children with death; and all the churches shall know that I am he which searcheth the reins, and hearts: and I will give unto every one of you according to your works."

29. A reference to the Bible, Dan. 5:18–28, in which a hand appears to the king Belshazzar and writes on the wall. Daniel agrees to interpret the writing, and his interpretation reads as follows:

O thou king, the most high God gave Nebuchadnezzar thy father a kingdom, and majesty, and glory, and honour: And for the majesty that he gave him, all people, nations, and languages, trembled and feared before him: whom he would he slew; and whom he would he kept alive;

and whom he would he set up; and whom he would he put down. But when his heart was lifted up, and his mind hardened in pride, he was deposed from his kingly throne, and they took his glory from him: And he was driven from the sons of men: and his heart was made like the beasts, and his dwelling was with the wild asses: they fed him with grass like oxen, and his body was wet with the dew of heaven; till he knew that the most high God ruled in the kingdom of men, and that he appointeth over it whomsoever he will. And thou his son, O Belshazzar, hast not humbled thine heart, though thou knewest all this; But hast lifted up thyself against the Lord of heaven; and they have brought the vessels of his house before thee, and thou, and thy lords, thy wives, and thy concubines, have drunk wine in them; and thou hast praised the gods of silver, and gold, of brass, iron, wood, and stone, which see not, nor hear, nor know: and the God in whose hand thy breath is, and whose are all thy ways, hast thou not glorified: Then was the part of the hand sent from him; and this writing was written. And this is the writing that was written, MENE, MENE, TEKEL, UPHARSIN. This is the interpretation of the thing: MENE; God hath numbered thy kingdom, and finished it. TEKEL; Thou art weighed in the balances, and art found wanting. PERES; Thy kingdom is divided, and given to the Medes and Persians.

30. From the Bible, 2 Sam. 22:30: "For by thee I have run through a troop; by my God have I leaped over a wall." This verse is repeated in Psalms 18:29.

31. From the Bible, Heb. 6:17-20: "Wherein God, willing more abundantly to show unto the heirs of promise the immutability of his counsel, confirmed *it* by an oath: That by two immutable things, in which *it was* impossible for God to lie, we might have a strong consolation, who have fled for refuge to lay hold upon the hope set before us; Which *hope* we have as an anchor of the soul, both sure and steadfast, and which entereth into that within the veil; Whither the forerunner is for us entered, *even* Jesus, made a high priest for ever after the order of Melchisedec."

32. In the nineteenth-century United States, the guillotine was commonly associated with the French Revolution (1789) and the Reign of Terror, in which many died by the guillotine.

33. From the Declaration of Independence.

34. Samuel Adams (1722–1803), the cousin of John Adams, was a leading patriot in the American Revolution.

35. The phrase "Rebellion to tyrants is obedience to God" is attributed to Puritan John Bradshaw (1602–59), president of the parliamentary commission that sentenced British king Charles I to death. Thomas Jefferson adopted the saying as his motto, and he and Benjamin Franklin proposed that it be included on the Great Seal of the United States.

WORKS CITED

Andrews, William L. *To Tell a Free Story: The First Century of Afro-American Autobiography, 1760–1865*. Urbana: University of Illinois Press, 1986.

Anglo-African Magazine, Volume 1—1859. Edited by William Loren Katz. New York: Arno Press and the New York Times, 1968.

Bibb, Henry. *The Life and Adventures of Henry Bibb, An American Slave, Written by Himself*. New York, 1850.

Billingsley, Andrew. *Mighty Like a River: The Black Church and Social Reform*. New York: Oxford University Press, 1999.

Blackett, R. J. M. *Building an Antislavery Wall: Black Americans in the Atlantic Abolitionist Movement, 1830–1860*. Ithaca: Cornell University Press, 1983.

Braxton, Joanne M. *Black Women Writing Autobiography: A Tradition within a Tradition*. Philadelphia: Temple University Press, 1989.

Brooks, Daphne A. *Bodies in Dissent: Spectacular Performances of Race and Freedom, 1850–1910*. Durham: Duke University Press, 2006.

Brooks, Elaine. "Massachusetts Anti-Slavery Society." *Journal of Negro History* 30, no. 3 (July 1945): 311–30.

Brown, William Wells. *A Lecture Delivered Before the Female Anti-Slavery Society of Salem, at Lyceum Hall, Nov. 14, 1847*. Boston: Massachusetts Anti-Slavery Society, 1847.

Byron, Gay L. *Symbolic Blackness and Ethnic Difference in Early Christian Literature*. London: Routledge, 2002.

Campbell, Stanley W. *The Slave Catchers: Enforcement of the Fugitive Slave Law, 1850–1860*. 1968. Reprint, New York: Norton, 1970.

Carey, Brycchan. *British Abolitionism and the Rhetoric of Sensibility: Writing, Sentiment, and Slavery, 1760–1807*. Houndmills, Basingstoke: Palgrave Macmillan, 2005.

Carwardine, Richard J. *Evangelicals and Politics in Antebellum America*. Knoxville: University of Tennessee Press, 1997.

"Celebration of W. I. Emancipation at Manchester, England." *Liberator*, 1 September 1854, 138–39.

Davis, Charles T., and Henry Louis Gates Jr., eds. *The Slave's Narrative*. Oxford: Oxford University Press, 1985.

Douglass, Frederick. *My Bondage and My Freedom*. 1855. In *Frederick Douglass: Autobiographies*, edited by Henry Louis Gates Jr. New York: Library of America, 1994.

———. *Narrative of the Life of Frederick Douglass, an American Slave*. 1845. In *Frederick Douglass: Autobiographies*, edited by Henry Louis Gates Jr. New York: Library of America, 1994.

———. "Self-Elevation—Rev. S. R. Ward." 1855. In *The Life and Writings of Frederick Douglass*, edited by Philip S. Foner, 2:359–62. New York: International Publishers, 1950.

———. "The Unholy Alliance of Negro Hate and Anti-Slavery." 1856. In *The Life and Writings of Frederick Douglass*, edited by Philip S. Foner, 2:385–87. New York: International Publishers, 1950.

Emerson, Ken. *Doo-Dah! Stephen Foster and the Rise of American Popular Culture*. Cambridge: Da Capo, 1998.

Ernest, John. *Liberation Historiography: African American Writers and the Challenge of History, 1794–1861*. Chapel Hill: University of North Carolina Press, 2004.

Fisch, Audrey. *American Slaves in Victorian England: Abolitionist Politics in Popular Literature and Culture*. Cambridge: Cambridge University Press, 2000.

———, ed. *The Cambridge Companion to the African American Slave Narrative*. Cambridge: Cambridge University Press, 2007.

Foner, Philip S., ed. *The Life and Writings of Frederick Douglass*. 5 vols. New York: International Publishers, 1950.

Foster, Frances Smith. *Witnessing Slavery: The Development of Ante-bellum Slave Narratives*. 1979. 2nd ed. Madison: University of Wisconsin Press, 1994.

Garnet, Henry Highland. "An Address to the Slaves of the United States of America." In *The Norton Anthology of African-American Literature*, edited by Henry Louis Gates Jr. and Nellie Y. McKay, 280–85. New York: Norton, 1997.

Gienapp, William E. "Abolitionism and the Nature of Antebellum Reform." In *Courage and Conscience: Black & White Abolitionists in Boston*, edited by Donald M. Jacobs, 21–46. Bloomington: Indiana University Press, 1993.

Gilroy, Paul. *The Black Atlantic: Modernity and Double Consciousness*. Cambridge: Harvard University Press, 1993.

Goldenberg, David M. *The Curse of Ham: Race and Slavery in Early Judaism, Christianity, and Islam*. Princeton: Princeton University Press, 2003.

Grimsted, David. *American Mobbing, 1828–1861: Toward Civil War*. New York: Oxford University Press, 1998.

Grover, Kathryn. *The Fugitive's Gibraltar: Escaping Slaves and Abolitionism in New Bedford, Massachusetts*. Amherst: University of Massachusetts Press, 2001.

Hartman, Saidiya V. *Scenes of Subjection: Terror, Slavery, and Self-Making in Nineteenth-Century America*. New York: Oxford University Press, 1997.

Hinks, Peter P. *To Awaken My Afflicted Brethren: David Walker and the Problem of Antebellum Slave Resistance*. University Park: Pennsylvania State University Press, 1997.

Hood, Robert E. *Begrimed and Black: Christian Traditions on Blacks and Blackness*. Minneapolis: Fortress Press, 1994.

Johnson, Sylvester A. *The Myth of Ham in Nineteenth-Century American Christianity: Race, Heathens, and the People of God*. New York: Palgrave Macmillan, 2004.

Knapp, Jacob. *Autobiography of Elder Jacob Knapp*. New York: Sheldon and Co.; Boston: Gould and Lincoln, 1868.

Lee, Debbie. *Slavery and the Romantic Imagination*. Philadelphia: University of Pennsylvania Press, 2002.

Litwack, Leon. "The Emancipation of the Negro Abolitionist." In *The Abolitionists*, edited by Richard O. Curry, 112–21. Hinsdale, Ill.: Dryden Press, 1973.

———. *North of Slavery: The Negro in the Free States, 1790–1860*. Chicago: University of Chicago Press, 1961.

Lorimer, Douglas A. *Colour, Class and the Victorians*. London: Leicester University Press, 1978.

Martineau, Harriet. *Retrospect of Western Travel*. 1838. Reprint, New York: Johnson Reprint, 1968.

McBride, Dwight A. *Impossible Witnesses: Truth, Abolitionism, and Slave Testimony*. New York: New York University Press, 2001.

Newman, Richard. Introduction to *Narrative of the Life of Henry Box Brown*, edited by Richard Newman, vii–xxxiii. Oxford: Oxford University Press, 2002.

"The Passenger in the Boot." *National Era*, 3 October 1850, 158.

Peabody, Ephraim. "Narratives of Fugitive Slaves." In *The Slave's Narrative*, edited by Charles T. Davis and Henry Louis Gates Jr., 19-28. Oxford: Oxford University Press, 1985.

Pease, William H., and Jane H. Pease. "Antislavery Ambivalence: Immediatism, Expediency, Race." In *Blacks in the Abolitionist Movement*, edited by John H. Bracey Jr., August Meier, and Elliott Rudwick, 95-107. Belmont, Calif.: Wadsworth Pub. Co., 1971.

Price, George R., and James Brewer Stewart. "Introduction: Hosea Easton and the Agony of Race." In *To Heal the Scourge of Prejudice: The Life and Writings of Hosea Easton*, ed. George R. Price and James Brewer Stewart, 1-47. Amherst: University of Massachusetts Press, 1999.

"The Reception at the Meionaon." *Liberator*, 20 October 1854, 166.

Richards, Leonard L. *"Gentlemen of Property and Standing": Anti-Abolition Mobs in Jacksonian America*. New York: Oxford University Press, 1970.

Ripley, C. Peter. Introduction to *The Black Abolitionist Papers*, vol. 1, *The British Isles, 1830-1865*, edited by C. Peter Ripley, 3-35. Chapel Hill: University of North Carolina Press, 1985.

Rohrbach, Augusta. *Truth Stranger Than Fiction: Race, Realism and the U.S. Literary Marketplace*. New York: Palgrave, 2002.

Ruggles, Jeffrey. *The Unboxing of Henry Brown*. Richmond: Library of Virginia, 2003.

Smith, Timothy L. *Revivalism & Social Reform: American Protestantism on the Eve of the Civil War*. San Francisco: Harper & Row, 1965.

Starling, Marion Wilson. *The Slave Narrative: Its Place in American History*. Washington, D.C.: Howard University Press, 1988.

Stearns, Charles. *Narrative of Henry Box Brown, Who Escaped from Slavery Enclosed in a Box 3 Feet Long and 2 Wide. Written from a Statement of Facts Made by Himself, With Remarks Upon the Remedy for Slavery*. Boston: Brown & Stearns, 1849.

Still, William. *The Underground Rail Road: A Record of Facts, Authentic Narratives, Letters, &c., Narrating the Hardships Hair-breadth Escapes and Death Struggles of the Slaves in their efforts for Freedom, as related by Themselves and Others, or Witnessed by the Author; Together with Sketches of Some of the Largest Stockholders, and Most Liberal Aiders and Advisers, of the Road*. 1872. Reprint, Ebony Classics, Chicago: Johnson Pub. Co., 1970.

Wolff, Cynthia Griffin. "Passing Beyond the Middle Passage: Henry 'Box' Brown's Translations of Slavery." *Massachusetts Review* 37 (Spring 1996): 23–44.

Wood, Marcus. *Blind Memory: Visual Representations of Slavery in England and America, 1780–1865*. New York: Routledge, 2000.

INDEX